# Bodies, Texts, and Ghosts

## *Writing on Literature and Law in Colonial Latin America*

Raúl Marrero-Fente

I0592432

University Press of America,® Inc.
Lanham · Boulder · New York · Toronto · Plymouth, UK

♾™ The paper used in this publication meets the minimum
requirements of American National Standard for Information
Sciences—Permanence of Paper for Printed Library Materials,
ANSI Z39.48-1992

A Conchita

# CONTENTS

# PREFACE

This book is oriented towards three research topics that are interrelated: epic poetry, spectral agency, and law in the Hispanic trans-Atlantic World during the colonial period. I have developed these research areas in the eleven chapters of this work by focusing on the cultural production of both sides of the Atlantic. The first five chapters of this study offer critical readings of several epic poems using the interdisciplinary approach of the phantom theory. *Bodies, Texts and Ghosts: Writing on Literature and Law in Colonial Latin America* offers new cultural readings of colonial texts by turning them away from the traditional interpretations that consider these works as mere appendices of a European tradition. Such readings constitute an example of how the field of colonial studies has moved away from historical readings towards more theoretical analysis, in tune with post-colonial studies and other critical orientations. In the first chapter, I express my debt to new critical thought, and present the theoretical approach that will guide this study. In the second chapter, I analyze *La Conquista del Perú* (1538) as a ghost text. The next chapter discusses haunting and violence as ideas that are crucial to the understanding of the poem, *Los actos y hazañasvalerosas del capitán Diego Hernández de Serpa* (1564), written by Pedro de la Cadena. In chapter 4, I examine the relationship between female agency and Amerindian ghosts in La *Araucana*(1569), a work devoted to the conquest of Chile. In the following chapter, I explore the concept of phantom authorship in *Nuevo Mundo y conquista* (1580), an epic poem by the Mexican author Francisco de Terrazas.

In chapter 6, I study the spectral presence in lyric poetry as depicted in the early romances narrating the conquest of Mexico. The focus of the next two chapters relies on the categories of phantom text, ghost author, and mourning to analyze the chronicles *Historia de la invención de lasIndias* (1525) by the Spanish author FernánPérez de Oliva, and *La Florida* (1605) by the Inca Garcilaso de la Vega. In the concluding three chapters of the book, I offer a systematic study of the literary and legal texts of Spain in the Americas by bringing together contemporary legal and cultural theory to the interpretation of this diverse corpus of writing. By focusing on the *Royal Commentaries* (1609) by the Inca Garcilaso de la Vega and other legal documents, I argue that this corpus of texts is also a narrative construct of cultural encounters. I examine the poetics of legal narrative by applying the theory of law as literature, a cross-disciplinary approach. I suggest that all the strategies and approaches developed in the field of colonial studies have neglected to examine this corpus of writings as cultural production. However, it is precisely rhetoric which provides an accessible medium for exploring the connection that exists between law and fiction.

The process of adapting the European models of writing contributed to the hybrid nature of the texts of the Spanish American encounter. This study demonstrates how an in-depth examination of this hybrid corpus of writings can enhance our understanding of the dynamic and complex character of the cultural production during colonial times. These new objects of study are works which pertain to discursive formations not considered strictly literary in the traditional sense. Accommodating an extraordinary range of information, these colonial texts became hybrids by encompassing many emerging fields of knowledge – such as law, history, geography and ethnography, among others—which would later become disciplines in their own right. Another essential factor contributing to the hybrid nature of these works was the frequent use by the authors of other textual models, such as: legal documents, philosophical writings, the novel of chivalry, epic and lyric poetry, and early travel accounts, just to name a few. Such models would allow these writers to couch the new in familiar terms, while simultaneously recurring to innovative textual strategies in order to relate their own particular stories. Hence, what my book proposes is a revision of the category of what we consider "colonial texts," and perhaps even more important, to explore the relationship that exists between literature and other types of discourses. The methodological consequences of this broadening of the range of objects of study represent an enrichment of perspectives in the field of colonial studies.

In several chapters of the book, I examine the varied formats adopted by early modern writing in Spain and the Americas: epic poetry, chronicles, legal documents, lyric poetry, and historical narratives. Through an interdisciplinary approach, I study how the different discursive formations of the colonial period represent racial, gender and cultural differences on both sides of the Atlantic. The texts of Colonial Latin America register the complex relations between European colonizers and non-European colonized people (Amerindians, mestizos, women, and African slaves), while also providing the foundation of today's understanding of the cultural legacy of the colonial era. My discussion will focus on how literary and legal texts incorporate the ways in which these works conceptualize, define, acquired knowledge, and control the other culture being represented. Colonial poetry and narrative then become a display of one culture in the act of representing another culture. This process entails an examination of the representation of cultural differences in colonial discourse.

In this book, I study legal discourse as central to the texts of the Spanish conquest of America, since law was the predominant discourse in the colonial period. Legal rhetoric was central to the works of the Spanish American encounter in yet another way. Many of these writings were motivated by the author's need to present his or her own life-story and legal cases in order to seek pardon, power or rewards for the services rendered to the Crown. The complexities of this corpus of writings derive from narrative strategies that respond to this dynamic of petition and persuasion. However, law remained the predominant mode of discourse during the colonial era. In the sixteenth century, the task of writing was subservient to the law: narrative, both fictional and historical, emerged within the forms and constraints of legal writing. Legal forms of discourse permeated the writing of history, while sustaining the idea of the Spanish empire in the Americas. In the prose of Renaissance historiography was couched the ideology of the conquering state, and the most sophisticated justifications for the conquest of the American territories were articulated.

My point is that colonial legislation in Spanish America can only be understood in its complexity when it is realized that legal discourse is not merely conceptual—that is, not reducible to a set of definitions—but also literary and cultural, by which I mean that its metaphorical, and associative quality derives precisely from the need to address the question of imposing principles of social control that are at the heart of any legislative controversy. In other words, the legislation of Spain in America should be studied not merely as a set of rules or institutions, but also as a kind of discursive practice of cultural dominance. This methodological approach is based on the assumption that a nexus between law and literature was at the center of the conquest of America.

Moreover, this work aims to promote the dialogue between Hispanic Atlantic cultures by exploring literature from a cross-cultural perspective, while also taking into account the theoretical contributions of spectral criticism. I argue that a transatlantic approach provides a broader framework to rethink the ways in which literature and culture has been formulated. In my view adopting a transatlantic perspective offers a method of thinking across geographical borders, which allow us to examine in-depth the reciprocal cultural exchange between Spain and its colonies during the 16th and 17th centuries. This innovative approach to Hispanic studies opens up new possibilities of interpretation, including the adoption of a global perspective in the field of Colonial Latin American studies.

*Bodies, Texts, and Ghosts: Writing on Literature and Law in Colonial Latin America*, examines the spectral presence in the texts of Colonial Latin America from an interdisciplinary perspective. I argue that spectral criticism offers the possibility of recovering the stories of violence, death, oppression, and injustice that come back from the past to remain with us in the present, and will reappear in the future as the legacies of colonialism. In other words, at the time of the expansion of the Spanish empire, the state developed discursive practices detailing ways to conquer, assimilate, transform or destroy the multiple ethnic groups within the territories occupied. In that sense, my project advocates for an ethical-oriented reading that takes into account the legacy of violence, and injustice that has prevailed in Latin America until the present. In my view, the analysis of colonial texts cannot be detached from today's social, political and cultural reality, which still bears the problems of a post-colonial society.

According to the spectral logic, ghosts do not only have the capacity to return from the past, but they are also waiting for us in the future. The aim of my study is precisely to go beyond the notion of the personal apparition of the ghost in order to explore the spectral trope in colonial discourse. Such critical approach is based upon the premise that the phantom metaphor is a productive one, since it suggests displaced, hidden or repressed ideas that appear in the colonial texts as well as in the critical studies. I apply the concept of spectral presence to the traces of violence, crime, and abuse that become visible in the writings of the colonial period. In this book, I argue that spectral criticism can be used to analyze the phantasmatic content repressed or marginalized in the texts of Colonial Latin America. This approach entails a reanimation of the category of the specter in the work of important contemporary thinkers. Spectral criticism is a recent theory stemming from studies by Giorgio Agamben, Judith Butler, Jacques Derrida, Jean-Claude Schmitt, Jean-Michel Rabaté, Stephen Greenblatt, David Punter, Nicolas Abraham, Maria Torok, Jean Laplanche, Michael Taussig, and Peter Buse. A recent trend in spectral criticism has been to examine the concepts of mourning, loss, and trauma simultaneously as is the case in the works by David Eng, David Kazanjian, Harrison Pogue, and AlessiaRicciardi.

Furthermore, my work stands at the center of a current debate concerning the significance of epic poetry as a means to understand the processes of cultural transfer, and exchange that took place between Spain and the Americas during the colonial period. The study of the epic genre must overcome the traditional scholarly barriers that separate the cultural production of early modern Spain and colonial Spanish America; since the notions of community and identity that emerged in the New World territories were the direct result of the transatlantic encounter that occurred in the 16th and 17th-centuries.

My study challenges the current understanding of epic poetry by suggesting that this literary genre is connected to both national (Spain) and local cultures (America). My purpose is to examine the rhetorical dimension of the epic poems as a process of emplotment of local communities in Colonial Spanish America. In my view, the theory and praxis of the Hispanic epic tradition is transatlantic in nature. This can be explained by the fact that the communities in Colonial Spanish America were the direct result of the transatlantic encounter that took place during the period of conquest and colonization of the Americas by the Spanish empire. By putting aside strict geographical boundaries my research intends to provide a new interpretative framework for this literary genre that will help to recover a neglected trans-Atlantic tradition of epic poetry, while also proposing a redefinition of the genre.

The book resituates the study of epic poetry by comparing texts written by peninsular as well as Creole authors, among them poems that narrate the conquest of the Caribbean, Mexico, Peru, Chile, Colombia, and Venezuela. Epic poetry was a literary genre that was overtly political, since it was linked to Spain's Imperial agenda: the politics of expansion and conquest of the Spanish empire during the 16th and 17th-century. I explore how the epic genre from both sides of the Atlantic represents cross-cultural encounters, that is, how different cultures, namely the Amerindian and European, meet, interact, and view one another. Therefore, epic poetry provides a textual representation of the unstable ground where cultures meet, and engage in a dynamic process of negotiation and confrontation. My work provides a new interpretative framework for the study of the Hispanic epic poetry by examining the "spectral trope" in colonial discourse. The development of the epic genre in the colonial period tells the story of the apparition of figures of phantasmagoria which stand at the center of these texts.

Finally, I will conclude by summarizing the contribution of my research to the renewal of the field of Latin American colonial studies. The purpose of this work is to open up a dialogue between the literary and legal texts written on both sides of the Atlantic, focusing on the processes of cultural transfer, and exchange that took place between Spain and its New World colonies during the 16th and 17th-centuries. Moreover, this book aims to provide a new interpretative framework for the study of this diverse corpus of writings by examining the "spectral trope" in colonial discourse. This approach to Hispanic studies is crucial to enhance our understanding of the dynamics and complex character of the cultural production that flourished during the colonial period; while also opening the way for the restoration of this cultural legacy from a global perspective.

## ACKNOWLEDGMENTS

I am grateful to the Program for Cultural Cooperation Between Spain's Ministry of Education, Culture and Sports, and United States' Universities, the Council for Research in the Humanities and Social Sciences at Columbia University, the Charles H. Watts Memorial Fellowship at the John Carter Brown Library, and the Mc Knight Summer Fellowship at the University of Minnesota for their support for this book. These grants allowed me to conduct research at the National Library and the National Archive in Madrid, Spain, the John Carter Brown Library, and other libraries in the United States, Latin America, and Spain. I also had the opportunity to conduct research as a Visiting Fellow at the Consejo Superior de Investigaciones Científicas in Madrid.

Armanda Lewis and Molly Leonard read the manuscript and made many comments and suggestions, and Raúl Rosales made a translation of chapter 1. I would like to thank all them for their support in this project. An earlier version of chapter 11 appeared as "Human Rights and Academic Discourse: Teaching the Las Casas-Sepúlveda Debate at the Time of the Iraq War." *Human Rights and Latin American Cultural Studies*. Ed. Ana Forcinito and Fernando Ordóñez. *Hispanic Issues On Line* 4.1 (2009): 247–259. I thank *Hispanic Issues On Line* for permission to published a revised version of this study.

# CHAPTER 1

## Spectral Agency: Epic, Loss and the Work of Mourning in Colonial Latin American Literature

To write today about epic poetry necessarily implies assuming a revisionist perspective in the field of colonial studies. Such a theoretical approach is based on the questioning of the prevailing ideas concerning the epic genre in colonial discourse. The progress achieved in the study of the chronicles of the conquest in recent years attests to the new vitality in the field of colonial studies. However, the exclusion of the epic genre from colonial studies has left a gap that must be filled in order to create a broader framework in which to view and analyze colonial writing in Latin America. The exclusion of epic from the diversity of critical approaches exemplifying recent advances in colonial studies has made it a ghost genre. The spectral dimension of epic poetry derives from the fact that it has been relegated to a marginal place within colonial discourse, since there are very few scholars who write about this genre nowadays. However, the epic genre is present in analyses concerning discursive formations, like the epic character of the chronicles of conquest. The most salient issue is that the main theme of the Conquest of America is precisely the heroic, depicted in the opposing forces of conquest and resistance; yet, until now colonial studies has analyzed this matter without taking into account the complexity that the epic genre brings to the field.

I apply this concept of "spectral presence" to the traces of violence, crime and abuse that appear in colonial discourse. In this study, I argue that spectral criticism can be used to analyze the phantasmatic content repressed or marginalized in the legal and literary texts of Colonial Spanish America. This entails a reanimation of the category of the specter in the work of important contemporary thinkers. Spectral criticism is a recent critical focus stemming from studies by Giorgio Agamben, Jacques Derrida, Jean-Claude Schmitt, Jean-Michel Rabaté, Stephen Greenblatt, Nicolas Abraham, Maria Torok, Jean Laplanche, Peter Buse, and Michael Taussig, among others. The work of these scholars demonstrates that the most productive encounters with ghosts do not take place in *séances*, but rather in the theoretical texts of philosophy, psychoanalysis, history and cultural and literary criticism. Therefore, spectral criticism offers the possibility of recovering the stories of violence, death, oppression and injustice that come back from the past, remain with us in the present and in the future: "Justice remains, is yet, to come, *a venir*," ("Force of Law" 27). In this sense, I also advocate here for an ethical-oriented reading that takes into account the legacy of injustice in Colonial Latin America. In other words, the presence of ghostly figures in any text breaks the logic of temporality while disrupting our sense of linear teleology. According to spectral logic, ghosts not only have the capacity to come from the past, but they are also waiting for us in the future. Since "...everything begins by the apparition of a specter. More precisely by the waiting for this apparition...the real nature of the "*revenant* is going to come" (Derrida 4).

This work is based on the idea that Epic Poetry in Colonial Spanish America constitutes "a series of accounts of the dead, but it is also a series of accounts by the dead" (Punter 262). Therefore, as Punter states, history must take into account the spectral presence, because the narratives of history cannot be written without them (262). This virtual dialogue is represented by Greenblatt "desire to speak with the dead"(*Shakespearean Negotiations...*1), and more recently his Hamlet in Purgatory. See also Michel de Certeau's analysis of Michelet's historiography and the concept of the sepulcher in *The Writing of History*. In any instance, that we encounter death we necessarily face loss, mourning and grief. If we consider loss as "what remains of it," then "the politics and ethics of mourning lies in the interpretation of what remains" (Eng and Kazanjian ix). Which in turn, allows us to develop an "spectral agency: one for whom a full "recovery" is not possible (Butler in Eng and Kazanjian 467). A recent tendency in spectral criticism is to study the topics of mourning, loss, and trauma together (Ricciardi 1-25).

I will refer to the main moments that pave the way for one form or another of the spectral in epic poetry. I should make clear that the passing from one moment to the next is relative and not absolute. A genealogy of the ghost in the epic is doubly elusive given the very characteristics of this poetic form-- denied, forgotten and always associated with death--with a time in the past that cannot return. The corpus of the sixteenth century colonial epic is formed by nine poems. I have devoted this study to the analysis of six of these texts, since these poems create a broader framework in which to view and explore the theoretical possibilities of spectral criticism. The history of the epic poetry of the colonial period recounts the emergence of figures of phantasmagoria that constitute this literary genre. Among these ghostly images is the foundational myth which establishes the origin of the colonial epic in 1569: the year that appeared the first part of Alonso de Ercilla's *La Araucana*, thus contributing to the idea of a false origin by disregarding other poems that were written before. As a result of this critical silence, certain poems were excluded from the teaching of epic poetry such as *Relación de la conquista y descubrimiento que hizo el Marqués don Francisco Pizarro en demanda de las provincias y rreynos que agora llamamos Nueva Castilla*, an anonymous work written between the years 1537 and 1538, which marks the transition of medieval epic models to American soil. The manuscript of this poem, a copy of the original text that was lost, is in Austria's National Library in Vienna. Unlike *La Araucana*, this anonymous poem still forms part of the medieval poetic tradition and is related to three works in particular: *Laberinto de Fortuna* by Juan de Mena, *Historia Parthenopea* by Alonso Hernández and *Historia de la Conquista de Orán y Jerusalén* by Martín de Herrera (Morton XLVI). There are no analyses of the relations between the medieval epic tradition and this epic poem based on the premise that there is an absolute epistemological discontinuity between the cultural productions in Spain and Spanish America. Such a theoretical approach does not take into consideration the existence of transatlantic connections between Europe and America since the year 1492. The poem can be classified as a "phantom text" due to two factors: first, from its disappearance among the manuscripts of the Library of Vienna until it was found in the nineteenth century, and subsequently published in 1848, and the text's anonymity. Within the tradition of Romantic criticism every text must be assigned an author, thus there was a prejudice against this anonymous poem. The critical studies of the period did not take into account the historical context of the production of this poem. Ironically, the most relevant aspect of this poem is not the author's identity or the reception of the text, but instead its own production. This work poses the theoretical question concerning the limits of the inter-discursive relations in an epic poem about the conquest of America; in particular it establishes the relation between History and Poetry. A book-seller from Lyon named J.A. Sprecher de Bernegg became the first editor of the poem and in his "Preface" to the edition published in Paris in 1848 he alludes to the spectral nature of the manuscript. The lack of a printed edition of the poem is described in a confidential tone, since it is depicted as a secret to be shared among a few scholars. The mystery of the fortuitous finding presents the poem as an apparition, in order words, as a specter that returns from the library shelves (without mentioning its name); and as a sort of gigantic tomb of knowledge. The disappearance of the text for years is one of the traits of the ghost text. The intervention by the editor discards the poem's original division in two parts and establishes a new division of five cantos, while adding a summary at the beginning of each canto. As a result of the editor's revision, the text is transformed into a Renaissance epic poem. In addition to its disappearance, this poem is a phantom text because it does not appear in literary histories, except for a brief mention in Pierce. The diversity of titles assigned to this epic poem increases the confusion surrounding this text. For example, sometimes it is referred to as *Conquista de la Nueva Castilla*, and at other times as *Conquista del Perú*. Furthermore, critics offer different assessments: for Menéndez Pelayo it is a poem written in *endecasílabo* verses; Rand Morton classified the work as a pre-Renaissance narrative poem; for Porras Barrenechea the poem is a rhymed chronicle; and according to Ticknor, the text constitutes a versified history.

Despite the 1848 edition by Bernegg, the poem continued to be an unknown and neglected text until the twentieth century, when it was re-edited by Morton in 1963 and by Coello in 2001. Both editions are bibliographic rarities, since Morton's edition is out of print, while the edition by Coello is difficult to find. The epic genre is cast by Morton as something dead and out-of-date. But in this poem there are aspects of the conquest of Peru that have not been explored in any of the first chronicles that narrate that historical event. Among the most important issues are those that refer to the itinerary of Pizarro's navigation and to the American territory; the unification of Pizarro's three voyages into two trips, which is narrated following the models of the medieval chronicles and the *portulano*; and, in my opinion the most relevant: a more complex picture of the encounter between Pizarro and Atahualpa in Cajamarca, which culminated with the Inca's death. The scene of the Cajamarca meeting in the poem offers unexplored aspects and details about this historic event that do not appear in the first chronicles of the conquest of Peru.

The First Part of *La Araucana* by Alonso de Ercilla (Madrid, 1533-1594) was published in Madrid in 1569, but the complete edition of the poem did not appear until 1597. *La Araucana* is a phantasmagoria of the epic genre, since in critical discourse this poem replaces the whole genre, the epic poetry of the colonial period. Any look at the bibliography of studies of Ercilla's text reveals the magnitude of the critical body of works devoted solely to the analysis of this poem. Therefore, an exclusionary tendency prevails in the field of colonial studies that is demonstrated by the lack of interest among scholars in studying other poems. Such critical blindness also results in a theoretical approach that looks only for themes and topics in *La Araucana* deriving from the classical epic tradition, transforming the poem into the only model of the colonial epic. As no in-depth work exists that covers the entire spectrum of epic poems written during the sixteenth and seventeenth centuries, the text of *La Araucana* can be placed at the center of a ghost canon.

From the opening canto *La Araucana* is defined as a poem of arms and heroes. But Ercilla immediately corrects the initial omission of the female presence in the poem by devoting various passages to women protagonists. The first heroine is Doña Mencía (canto VII), a Spanish woman, who inverts the traditional gender codes in society and assumes an extraordinary leading role in the battlefield. However, the reference to several Amerindian heroines throughout the poem is one of the most salient aspects of this text. For example, the second female character mentioned in canto XIII is the Amerindian Guacolda, who along with her husband Lautaro dreams of his death. Soon after, in canto XX of the second part, another Amerindian heroine appears: Tegualda, who resembles a ghost searching at night for her husband's remains. The description of this spectral figure includes all the elements associated with a ghost: the dark night, the difficult vision, the wariness, the sighs, the fear, the cries, and the appearance of another sentinel as eyewitness. In canto XXVIII of the Second Part, Ercilla continues with his portrayal of Glaura. This Amerindian woman explains how she lost her husband Cariolano during a combat against the Spanish army, and describes their fortuitous encounter. Canto XXXII of the Third Part is devoted to the Amerindian character of Lauca, who also lost her husband in battle. The ghostly figure of Lauca is depicted in the poem as wearing white clothes tainted with blood. Lauca has been wounded during the war and roams alone looking for her beloved. This Amerindian heroine becomes an example of conjugal fidelity beyond death and serves as a predecessor to the tragic story of Dido (Schwartz Lerner 615-625). The tale of Dido narrated in chapters XXXII and XXXIII is the apotheosis of a female character who sacrifices herself for love. One must try to answer the question of why the capture of Caupolicán appears in the same chapter. The poem's stories about

Amerindian heroines represent the ghost figure because the female characters are always portrayed in connection with death. But the spectral figure has another significance in the poem, since it can also be read as an allegory of what remains outside, of something that cannot be stated or defined, and of everything that is exceptional and extraordinary. The feminine episodes of *La Araucana* recall the ghost's category pertaining to theoretical discourse, which is defined by Rabaté as less the result of the loss of an object than an awareness that this object was always destined to be vanished due to its exceptional quality (xxii). The feminine presence in *La Araucana* constitutes an exceptional element of the epic tradition of the colonial period, and deserves closer attention and a systematic reappraisal of the role of lament and the poetics of loss in epic poetry from a feminist perspective, as has occurred in the works of Elaine Fanthan, Sheila Murnaghan, and Victoria Pagán dedicated to the study of classical epic.

*Nuevo Mundo y conquista* was written by Francisco de Terrazas, a Mexican writer who was born before 1549 and who died in 1600. Terrazas was also the author of several lyrical poems collected in *Flores de varia poesia*, published in Mexico in 1577, and of other poems. The Mexican writer figures as one of the Spanish-American authors praised by Cervantes in "Canto a Calíope" (Peña 8-12). *Nuevo Mundo y conquista* is inserted into the text of the *Sumaria Relación de las cosas de la Nueva España con noticia individual de los descendientes legítimos de los conquistadores y primeros pobladores españoles*, written by Baltasar Dorantes de Carranza in 1604, but published in 1902. Hence, the readers of Terrazas's poem inherited a mediated, unfinished and fragmented text. In his chronicle, Dorantes states that Terrazas passed away before he was able to finish his work. On the other hand, the delay in the publication of Dorantes's *Sumaria Relación* contributed to the scholars' neglect of this epic poem until the twentieth century. The exception was the appearance of a limited edition by Icazbalceta at the end of the nineteenth century. But *Nuevo Mundo y conquista* can be considered a phantom text, since even though it was a relatively unknown poem at the time, it had a decisive influence on other epic poems that were published later, such as: *Cortés valeroso* (1588) *y Mexicana* (1594) by Gabriel Lobo Lasso de la Vega and *El Peregrino indiano* by Antonio Saavedra (1599). The original manuscript by Terrazas remains lost and the only available copy is an incomplete version of the poem. Dorantes inserts twenty-three fragments of Terrazas's poem into his own text, identifying the author in certain passages while in other sections, he remains uncertain. In Dorantes' chronicle the autorship is shared by lesser known poets, among them José de Arrázola, Salvador de Cuenca and Alonso Pérez. The sequence of ghost authors is the most salient aspect of the text, but in addition to the question of authorship we must also take into account the fragmentary nature of the work. Terrazas's text is altered by Dorantes who inserts the fragments of the epic poem according to the reading order of his own chronicle; that is, he first quotes a passage of the text that should come later, changing the original plan of the poem. All the available editions of *Nuevo Mundo y conquista* are readings, based solely on speculations, as no original manuscript of the poem is known to exist. Therefore, every study about the poem must begin with a phantom text and a ghost authorship, and any theoretical approach applied to the analysis of this work will be an example of spectral criticism. The scholar must decide whether we should read the poem within its context, that is, from the *Sumaria Relación*, as a text that serves to validate the work of Dorantes, or as a series of isolated fragments. Terrazas dedicates a passage of his poem to the idyll of an indigenous couple, Quetzal and Huitzel, who are separated from each other by the conquest. In the verses that describe the capture of Huitzel and the farewell of the lovers, the figure of the ghost emerges as the central image of the passage. After being captured, Huitzel promises that she will return as a spirit and shadow to see him again:

> Si voy para vivir puesta en servicio
> tenerme ha tu memoria compañía,
> y en un continuo y solitario oficio
> llorando pasaré la noche y día;
> mas si muriendo en triste sacrificio
> fortuna abrevia la desdicha mía,
> adonde estés vendré, no tengas duda,
> espíritu desnudo y sombra muda (Terrazas 37).

> [If I am going to live placed in servitude
> may memories of you keep me company,
> and in continuous and solitary work
> I will be crying all day and night;
> but if dying in sad sacrifice
> fortune lessens my misfortune,
> wherever you are I will come, do not doubt it,
> naked spirit and mute shadow]

Terrazas borrowed this ghost figure from the tradition of phantasmal images of heroic love that appear in lyric poetry, such as the French romances, Provençal poetry, and Petrarch's *Rime in morte di Madonna Laura;* and also in Dante's *Commedia* (Agamben 71-76; Gargano 181-220). In the most comprehensive study about the ghost figure in the medieval imaginary, the historian Jean Claude Schmitt states that the phantom as an invisible image (as we identify it today) is already present in the thirteenth century in two stories from the *Cantigas de Santa María*: Cantiga CXXIII and Cantiga LXXII (210). Although the presence of these phantasmal images in lyric poetry is undeniable, Terrazas's passage also recalls the ghost of Creusa, Aeneas's wife in *The Aeneid.* The appropriation of the ghost image in the verses of Terrazas's poem, "adonde estés vendré / no tengas duda, espíritu desnudo y sombra muda" ["wherever you are I will come, do not doubt it, naked spirit and mute shadow"], not only establishes the cross-boundary of literary genres (lyric and epic poetry), it also has the power to evoke. The figure of the ghost with its evocative capacity functions as an allegory of the epic genre, since it alludes to the disappearance and neglect of this subject from the theoretical discourse of colonial studies. But at the same time, it is a powerful image that announces the return of the ghost. In other words, it is a silencing presence that persists in other genres because the spectral figure is also a metaphor that evokes the exchange that takes place between discursive genres and the cross-cultural encounters between the European and the Amerindian cultures.

The *Primera Parte de las Elegías de varones ilustres de Indias* by Juan de Castellanos (Alanís, Seville, 1522-Tunja, Colombia, 1607) was published in Madrid in 1589. The elegies are divided into four parts that comprise a total of 113,000 verses, but only the *Primera Parte* appeared during Castellanos' life. The rest of the work began to be published in 1847 and the first complete edition dates from 1930-32. Castellanos worked for a period of over ten years on the versification of this chronicle. The manuscript of the elegies, initially written in prose, disappeared. Because of its discursive complexity this work is considered an encyclopedic account of the culture of the period. In the poem there are different literary and non-literary discursive forms, such as eulogies, elegies, eclogues, catalogues, romances, pilgrimages and accounts. Castellanos's poem has antecedents in *Generaciones y semblanzas* by Fernán Pérez de Guzmán and *Claros varones de Castilla* by Fernando del Pulgar (Restrepo 29-71). Among the various discursive forms in Castellanos's poem is the elegy, a poetic form dedicated to the lament over death; as a result, the *Primera Parte* is transformed into an extended elegy. Of the fourteen cantos there are twelve elegies devoted to the death of several conquistadors, among them: Rodrigo de Arana (II), Francisco de Bobadilla (III), Christopher Columbus (IV), Diego Columbus (V), Juan Ponce de León (VI), Diego Velázquez (VII), Francisco de Garay (VIII), Diego de Ordás (IX), Jerónimo de Ortal (XI), Antonio de Sedeño (XII), Diego de Ursúa and Lope de Aguirre (XIV). The rhetoric of Castellanos's mourning is already depicted in the poem's exordium of the first canto, where in a confidential tone he declares:

> A cantos elegíacos levanto
> Con débiles acentos voz anciana,
> Bien como blanco cisne que con canto
> Su muerte soleniza ya cercana:
> No penen mis amigos con espanto,
> Por no lo comenzar mas de mañana;
> Pues suelen diferir buenos intentos
> Mil varios y diversos corrimientos.
>
> Para dar órden á lo prometido,
> Orbe de Indias es el que me llama
> A sacar del sepulcro del olvido
> A quien merece bien eterna fama:
> Diré lo que me fuere permitido
> Por la que descompone nuestra trama,
> Pues para correr vias tan distantes
> Había de tomallas mucho antes (Castellanos XXX).

[To chants of elegy I raise
An ancient voice with weak accents,
Willingly like a white swan that with song
Solemnizes its death already near:
Do not suffer my friends with fear,
For not commencing it tomorrow;
For good intentions tend to differ
A thousand various and diverse paths.

In order to fulfill what has been promised,
The world of the Indies calls me
To remove from the sepulcher of neglect
He who well deserves eternal fame:
I will state what is allowed of me
By which our plot is unsettled,
For to undertake such distant paths
I should have taken them much earlier.]

Although the topics of the memory remind us of Ercilla's declaration, there is a subtle distinction with Castellanos mourning, since he uses the sepulcher in his poem as a *locus* of enunciation. In other words, the act of evoking the deceased takes place from death itself: the loss of friends in battle and the authors' proximate experience of his own death. From Castellanos's poem, I will analyze one example of the work of mourning from Elegy VI, dedicated to the conquest of Puerto Rico and to the historical figure of Juan Ponce de León:

Algo fue rojo, de gracioso gesto,
Afable, bien querido de su gente,
En todas proporciones bien compuesto,
Sufridor de trabajos grandemente,
En cualesquier peligros el mas presto,
No sin estremos grandes de valientes,
Enemigo de amigos de regalos,
Pero muy envidiado de los malos (Castellanos XX)

[Somewhat fair-skinned, of graceful face,
Affable, much-loved by his people,
In all proportions well-built,
A great bearer of labors,
The quickest in any dangers,
Not without great extremes of the courageous,
Enemy of friends of gifts,
But very envied by the wicked.]

Funeral ceremony:

Todos aquellos hombres principales,
Vecinos de la isla Fernandina,
Solenizaron estos funerales,

Con gran autoridad y pompa dina,
Segun las cermonias de los tales
Al tiempo que al sepulcro se camina:
Y en el túmulo alto que tenia
Un dístico pusieron que decia:
*Epitafio*

Aqueste lugar estrecho
Es sepulcro del varon,
que en el nombre fue Leon
Y mucho mas en el hecho (Castellanos XX).

[All those illustrious men,
Residents of the island of Fernandina,
Solemnized these funerals,
With great authority and fitting pomp,
According to ceremonies of this type
When walking to the sepulcher:
And in the high tumulus that it had
Was placed a distich that read:
*Epitaph*

This narrow space
Is the sepulcher of the man,
Who in name was Lion
And much more in action.]

The structure of the elegy includes a description of the hero with his most salient physical and moral characteristics; this functions as an evocation of the dead and at the same time it gives corporality to the spirit, which becomes a specter (Derrida, *Work of Mourning* 72). This is the first instance of the return of the ghost. Each elegy concludes with a funeral scene that functions as the instant of departure: the farewell of the dead friend who leaves, and an epitaph that summarizes the person's life in one sentence. The memorial of the lost friend is a gesture of evocation that made the ghost come back. In mourning we must realize that the dead person is now inside of us ("in us") and at the same time the lost one becomes only an image for us, since the dead in his/her "infinite alterity" is beyond our reach (Derrida, *Work of Mourning* 11). We must bear in mind that the function of the mourning ritual is precisely to ontologize the mortal remains, that is, first to make them present, and then to identify and localize the body (Derrida, *Work of Mourning* 11). In his epic poem, Castellanos follows the mourning ritual when he describes each of the dead conquistadores, recalls the funeral and, finally, depicts the tomb and the epitaph, as the site where the body is buried. Castellano's mourning ritual, portrait of the heroes, burial of the dead and epitaph of the tomb derives from a social imaginary: the tales and images of the apparition of the ghost in dreams which along with the socialized discourse of the sermon and mourning have contributed to the creation of images, tales and shared beliefs concerning this subject that have been transmitted from generation to generation (Schmitt 10). This reminds us of one of the oldest tales of apparitions of the dead in dreams: that of the spirit of Patroclus to his friend Achilles. In this Homeric tale of the ghost pursuing the living, an inversion of reality takes place when the living appropriates the voices of the dead; that is, when the living makes the voice of the spirit his own, a stronger voice now emerges based on a supernatural source. The authority conferred by the apparition of the ghost not only legitimizes the poetic voice, but it also grants immortality to his work. Therefore, it can be concluded that in this gesture of the appropriation of the spirit's voice, it is the living who gives the dead a sort of postmorten existence (Schmitt 224). With the gallery of famous figures from the conquest of America that he included in his epic poem, Castellanos was able to establish a voice of extraordinary authority. This infinite muttering of the voices of the dead conquistadores, who always return from their adventures and pursue the writer with the memories of their deeds, constitutes the primary source of the author's strength. Castellanos chooses the elegy to evoke the deceased heroes, because the realm of the dead is the ultimate space of enunciation, since it confers the greater source of authority to the poetic voice. The central image of the poem is death, both as a personal experience and as a communal experience, the condition of mortality of all human beings. In Castellanos's epic poem, the stories about the dead Spanish conquistadores are combined with accounts of indigenous people and episodes of deaths in battlefields. In a recent essay, Thomas Greene emphasizes the ability of the epic to convey a sense of community among the members of a group of people who share the same pain. Greene refers to this quality as "the natural tears of the epic," which he defines as the deep commitment of epic poetry to express the pain and ritual of death (189). Hence, we can state that the figure of the ghost is the primary trope of Castellanos's work, since his own poetic voice is described as the voice of the dying, and all of the heroes evoked in the poem inhabit the realm of the dead.

The epic poem *Primera Parte de Cortés valeroso y Mexicana* written by Gabriel Lobo Lasso de la Vega (1588-1615) was published in Madrid in 1588. The poem is divided into twelve cantos and 1,115 octaves. Eight years later, in 1594 another work appeared in Madrid titled *Mexicana de Gabriel Lobo Lasso de la Vega, enmendada y añadida por su mismo autor*, which was a rewriting of the original poem of 1588. The second poem consists of twenty-five cantos and 1,682 octaves. These two poems by the same author can be considered commissioned works written at the request of the Cortés family and form part of the so-called Cortés cycle, since they present an idealized and glorious portrait of Hernán Cortés. They seek to create a glorious image of the conquistador of Mexico in order to support the demands of his criollos descendents. In this study, I will not examine Cortés's ghost and its relevance for the agenda of reclamations of the *criollos*; instead, I will focus on the relations that exist between the specter and property but from the indigenous perspective. The apparition of the Amerindian ghost allegorizes the fear felt by the criollo society established in Spanish America of the pre-Colombian past and of the subversive forces of indigenous cultures. Unlike the other apparitions in the epic poem – among them, the apostle James, the Virgin, the angel Michael and other angels – there is an apparition of the dead in canto XII of *Primera Parte de Cortés valeroso y Mexicana* (1588) of great symbolism. I am referring to the scene that narrates the return from the otherworld of the ghost of Acamapich to warn the emperor Montezuma of his weakness when confronting the Spanish conquistadors. In the following verses, Lobo Lasso describes in detail the apparition of the Amerindian spirit:

> Estando solo Motezuma un día,
> cuidoso a un aposento retirado,
> todo el suelo sintió se estremecía,
> de que quedó confuso y espantado;
> vio una fogosa boca en él se abría,
> y por ella salir un hombre armado;
> de aspecto fiero, bravo y vista horrible,
> que con voz le amenaza, cruel, terrible.
>
> De fea amarillez cubierto el gesto,
> y de mortal tiniebla, triste, escura;
> con visaje espantable, descompuesto,
> descarnado y de fiera catadura;
> causole a Motezuma terror esto,
> y más cuando una llama viva y pura,
> vido que por los ojos le salía,
> y el turbio y negro aliento que esparcía.
>
> Erízasele al Rey turbado el pelo,
> y el fatigado aliento le faltaba;
> un entrañable miedo y frío yelo
> los miserables huesos le ocupaba;
> tiembla los ojos puestos en el suelo,
> que a la fiera visión mirar no osaba;
> la cual le dice: "Tímido, abatido,
> indigno del estado que has tenido.
>
> "Yo soy Acamapich, que la corona
> gran tiempo tuve deste triste estado
> que agora el español falso pregona
> haber con fuerte diestra sujetado.
> Este reedificó mi real persona
> para que tú, imprudente, acobardado,
> vinieses a perder con flaca mano,
> y su temido nombre el mexicano.
>
> "¿Quién sino tú, en su reino, entre su gente
> a un estranjero triste se rindiera
> y a la dura prisión infamemente

la cerviz libre y yerta sometiera?
¿O quién a Qualpopoca un tal pariente,
quemar ante sus ojos consintiera?
¿O quién su antigua ley no sustentara,
antes muriendo, que otro se sembrara?

"Del reino escuro y cárcel tenebrosa
a que me condenó mi adverso hado,
vengo sólo a avisarte de una cosa,
de tu infelice suerte latismado,
y es que esta gente brava, cauta, odiosa,
mates o envíes luego de tu estado,
sino quieres perderle con la vida,
en abatida y mísera caída".

Desapareció el demonio con aquesto,
que habla en forma de aquél aparecido;  (Pulles Linares 780-782)


[Being Montezuma alone one day,
retired to a secluded place,
he felt the whole earth tremble,
and was confused and frightened;
and he saw an ardent opening of the ground,
and an armed man come out of it;
of an alarming appearance, violent and a horrible sight,
who with his voice threatened, cruelly, terribly.

His face covered by an ugly yellowness,
and a great darkness, gloomy, obscure;
with a frightening grimace, impudent,
fleshless and with a savage countenance;
this caused terror in Montezuma,
and more so when an intense and sheer flame,
he saw coming out of his eyes,
and the turbid and black breath that was dispersed.

The hair of the disturbed King set on end,
and he could not catch his fleeting breath;
a deep fear and a cold chill
took hold of his miserable bones;
he shuddered with his eyes fixed on the ground,
and did not dare to look at the savage vision;
which spoke to him: "Timid, dejected,
unworthy of the position you hold.

"I am Acamapich, whose crown
of this sad state I long held
which now the false Spaniard proclaims
to have grasped with a strong right hand.

My true personage was rebuilt
so that you, imprudent, intimidated,
would come to lose with weak hand,
and his feared name the Mexican.

"Who if not you, in his kingdom, among his people
would surrender to a worthless foreigner
and to a harsh prison would vilely
submit your stiff and free neck?
Or who to Qualpopoca a said relative,
would allow to be burned before his eyes?
Or who would not uphold his ancient law,
dying before it is trampled by another?

From the dark kingdom and gloomy jail
to which my adverse fate condemned me,
I come only to warn you of one thing,
wounded by your unfortunate luck,
and it is that these violent, sly, hateful people,
you kill or expel from your state,
unless you want to lose it with life,
in a humiliating and miserable fall."

With this the demon disappeared,
who had appeared in this form].

The passage quoted above refers to the apparition of the spirit of Acamapixtli, a former Aztec ruler whose name means "handful of stalks." In his chronicle, Sahagún states that "he was the first lord of Mexico, of Tenochtitlan, and had dominion over Mexico for twenty-one peaceful years and there were no wars during his reign" (Pullés 216). The apparition of the ghost of Acamapich is a strong image that suggests the possible danger of going back to the times when the Amerindian lived according to their own rules and customs, since one of the traits of the specter is its temporal simultaneity. In other words, the phantom that returns from the past is also the messenger of the future because this figure has the power of making demands whose later consequences could alter the times yet to come. The dispossessed Amerindian will demand the return of the land that was taken away from them by the Spaniards. It is also an allegory of the apprehension among the descendants of the conquistadors of the possible illegal nature of their own claims. Furthermore, the importance of Acamapich's ghost is that it also represents the legal concept of ownership. The allegory of the Aztec phantom in the epic poem reminds us that, in the act of taking possession of the land, the conquistadors and their descendants have been haunted by the ghosts that inhabit the territory they now claim to have conquered. The apparition of the ghost of Acamapich foretells the conquistador's duty regarding the native's demands for the dispossession of their lands. It is no coincidence that the claims to ownership of the land appeal ultimately to the dead ancestors, as the most important source of legality.

The epic poem *El peregrino indiano* by Antonio de Saavedra Guzmán was published in Madrid in 1599. The poem, which is divided into twenty cantos and 2,036 octaves is considered the most detailed work of the Cortés cycle that was written during the sixteenth century. In addition, there are certain passages in this poem that are similar to Terrazas' and Lobo Lasso de la Vega's works. Several scholars who have studied the poem (such as García Icazbalceta, Amor y Vázquez, Margarita Peña, and the most recent editor José Rubén Romero Galván) agree that this work is an account of the merits and services rendered to the Spanish Crown of a *criollo,* who was unsatisfied with his social status. In canto IX of the poem the Amerindian woman called Tlantepuzylama acts as a conjurer who casts an incantation, establishing a communication between the world of the living and the realm of the dead.

> En este punto vino una Agorera
> De gran reputación, industria, y fama
> Sutil, astuta, y diestra hechicera,
> Que entre ellos llaman Tlantepuzylama:
> Dixo a Maxixcaltzin, que justo fuera
> Que pues la guerra tanto se derrama,
> Se huuiera su consejo procurado,
> Pues sabe quanto en todo es acertado.
>
> ............................................
>
> Sacó tres candelillas muy delgadas
> Y estandolas muy passo conjurando
> En tierra las rodillas humilladas,
> Con el baho las fue viuificando:
> Echaua del ardientes llamaradas,
> Con que las escendio, y quedo temblando,
> Afligida, cansada, y denegrida,
> Que huuiera de perder alli la vida.
>
> Luego tomó el peyote muy molido,
> Desatado en vna agua delicada,
> De confecciones de aguas de oluido,
> Y del Leteo estigie emponçoñada:
> Beuiole, y al passar le dio vn gemido,
> Y vna terrible y rezia dentellada,
> Y alçando el dedo con el braço todo,
> Hizo conuocaciones deste modo.
>
> ............................................
>
> Obedeced mi mando establecido,
> Haciendo aquí patente en un momento

cuanto en el mundo todo ha sucedido,
Y en la esfera del alto fundamento:
Mostradme aquí muy claro y conocido
Lo porvenir, pasado y el intento
Desta gente de España, y su venida,
Para que sea patente y entendida (Saavedra y Guzmán 265-66).

[At this point came a Seer
Of great reputation, industriousness, and fame
A keen, astute and skilled conjurer
Who among themselves they call Tlantepuzylama:
She said to Maxixcaltzin that it was understood
As the war was so widespread,
That her advice was requested,
For he knows how right she is in all.

She took out three very thin candles
And holding them started the spell
On the ground with moist knees,
With the earth she brought them to life:
It emitted strong flames,
With which she lit them, and remained trembling,
Afflicted, tired, and denigrated
That she would lose her life there.

She then took the very-crushed *peyote*
Dissolved in a delicate water,
Concocted from other waters,
And poisoned from the infernal Leteo:
She drank it, and as she passed by let out a sigh,
And a terrible and rough bite,
And raising her finger with the whole arm,
She spoke in the following manner.

Obey my established command,
Making patent here at this moment
What has taken place in all the world,
And in the sphere of the highest principle:
Show me here very clearly and known
The future, past and the intention
Of these people from Spain, and their coming,
So it may be patent and understood.]

After casting the spell, Tlantepuzylama has a vision of the fatal outcome of
the war for her people and the desolation awaiting Tlaxcala; thus, she decides to
advise Maxixcatzin, the Tlaxcalan ruler, that he should make peace with the
Spaniards. In this passage Romero sees influences of *Orlando Furioso* and of
*Pharsalia*, where there is also an enchanting witch character. In these influences
he also sees a product of the author's *criollismo*, personified by the character of

Tlantepuzylama (Romero Galván, *Tlantepuzylama* 124). The Amerindian sorceress also plays the role of the phantasm in the poem, because she descends to the world of the dead and later returns to the realm of the living in order to deliver her prophetic message to her people. Tlantepuzylama, in order to communicate with the spirits, must cease to act as the living and pretend to have become a specter herself; that is, she has to enter into a common condition with the dead (Ogden 253). However, in order to act like a specter, Tlantepuzylama must transform her own appearance to imitate the figure of the ghost. On the other hand, the scene that describes the incantation of the Amerindian sorceress changes the main objective of the poem: to glorify the heroic figure of Hernán Cortés and the Spanish conquistadors to support the claims made by the criollos. Tlantepuzylama's prophecy replaces the vision of the conquest of Mexico as a heroic deed of the Spaniards with the idea that the conquest was not a heroic effort of epic dimensions, but rather an act of destruction.

To conclude, we can state that the ghost is an antidote against the closed ending, against the exhaustion of theoretical discourse, as there is always the possibility of going further, of expanding the horizon. The spectral is what cannot be contained, restricted, stopped or exhausted. It is the very nature of thought, always searching for something new, the infinite and never-ending process from one generation to the next. In the poems examined we have seen how the specter serves as a metaphor to help us to understand the complex transatlantic exchange that took place between the Spanish and the Amerindian cultures; and between the texts and agency of Spain and the Americas. If we place the ghost metaphor at the center of our analysis of epic poetry, we can arrive at a better understanding of the richness and complexity of the epic poems from the colonial period.

# CHAPTER 2

## Phantom Texts, Scientific Knowledge and Cultural Geography in *La Conquista del Perú (1538)*

Most studies on Spanish Golden Age epic poetry established the birth of the genre after the debate created by the "discovery" of Aristotle's *Poetics*. This *loci* in literary historiography does not, however, take into account other important aspects, including the composition of epic poetry prior to this event. It is necessary to consider the broad history of translations and editions of the *Poetics*, which begin at the end of the Middle Ages and culminate with the 1508 edition of Aldo Manuzio, and extend to the critical debate beginning in 1548, the year which marked the beginning of reviews by Robortello. This commentary renewed the history of the epic genre and exerted an influence beyond Robortello's time and beyond Italy. Echoes of the neoaristotelian debate fashioned a particular image in literary historiography lasting up to the twentieth century, in which the importance of theoretical discourse on creative work was favored. An example of the consequences of this debate appears in the classic study by Frank Pierce, *The Spanish Epic Poetry of the Golden Age*. Pierce establishes the periodization of epic poems starting from the *Christo Pathia* of Juan de Quirós (1552), and the history of criticism beginning from the *Arte poética en verso castellano* by Miguel Sánchez de Lima (Alcalá de Henares, 1580), despite the fact that there were other important treaties before that date, including *In artem poeticam* by Brocense (Salamanca, 1558), *De Oratione* by Antonio Lulio (appearing before 1554), and even older treaties such as *Veritas fucata, sive de licentia poetica* Luis Vives (1523) and other non-extant texts.

The most important consequence of this disconnect in critical discourse is that it promotes the idea that there are no epic poems before 1550, and thus presents the epic genre as it were a mere appendix to the post-Aristotelian debate. Ignoring the history of earlier criticism of the *Poetics* by excluding important remarks as those of Vida in 1527, this approach takes into account only works that meet the standards set out from the debate among neoaristotelics critics and. The "there are no poetry without poetics" formula makes any elaboration on the history of the genre problematic. It is necessary to reiterate that within the apparent doctrinal vacuum that existed before the recovery of the *Poetics*, there was a set of outstanding works and treaties that disseminated poetic ideas from the classical tradition, including works by Horace, Cicero and Quintilian, and from the medieval period. From the Middle Ages it is worth mentioning San Isidore's *Etymologies* (VIII, 7, 10), from which "the history-poetry distinction continued for a long time," and spread to the works of Dante, Boccaccio, Petrarch, and other European authors. To this diffusion must be added the very practice of Spanish authors, exemplified by the *Arte de trovar* of Enrique de Villena, *La Gaya ciencia* by Guillén of Segovia, the "Foreword" to the *Cancionero* by Juan Alfonso de Baena (1445), the *Prohemio* of the Marquis de Santillana (1446-49), and the *Arte de poesía* by Juan del Encina (1496).

It is overlooked that one essential aspect in the creation of the norms of the epic genre corresponds to the influence of the classical models and their translations, commentaries and interpretations that originate from the Middle Ages. These include such works as the glosses to the *Aeneid* by Enrique de Villena (1427-28), the first Spanish version of the *Iliad* requested by the Marquis de Santillana (ca. 1446-1452), and translations of the *Iliad* by Juan de Mena (1519), the *Aeneid* by Francisco de las Natas (1528), and the *Farsalia* by Martin Lasso de Oropesa (1530), among others. There is a need, however, to clarify that the dissemination of such translations was not always comprehensive, and that some of these works were not known at the time.

To this panorama of literary history must be added the production of Spanish poetry in the fourteenth century, a time when Spain observed an emergence of chronicles in verse that embraced the *copla de arte mayor* as their metric structure. This heroic narrative poetry, named "new epic" by Alan Deyermond and Mercedes Vaquero, has major differences with the previous medieval epic, including the adoption of the *copla de arte mayor* as a reaction to the *cuaderna vía* and the use of a historicity which countered poetry that celebrated distant events. An important example of this type of work is the *Poema de Alfonso XI* of Rodrigo Yáñez, composed in 1348 and dedicated to celebrate the war effort of the *Reconquista* with the exaltation of a historic present. Named by Pedro M. Cátedra "historiography in verse", this new poetic tradition includes "historical poems and chronicles in verse" and highlights the permeability of a mixed genre, which counts among its most prominent ancestors the *Farsalia* of Lucano. In this new poetic modality belong such works as the missing chronicles of Hernardo de Ribera and the *Coplas de la batalla de la vega de Antequera* by Juan Galindo, both of which are part an extensive body of work that includes: *El cancionero* by Pedro Marcuello, *Panegírico en alabanza de la reyna Isabel* by Diego Guillén de Ávila (1499), *Obra compuesta para el arzobispo Carrillo* by Guillén de Segovia, *Excelencias de la reina Isabel* by Pedro de Gracia Dei, *Doce triunfos de los doce apostóles* of Juan de Padilla, *Laberinto del Marques de Cadiz* (1493), *Prácticas de las virtudes de los Buenos reyes d'España en coplas de arte mayor* by Francisco de Castilla (1517), *Vida rimada of Fernán Gonzalez* by Gonzalo Arredondo, *Consolatoria de Castilla* by Juan de Barba (1493), *Ystorias de la divinal vitoria y nueva acquisición de la muy insigne cibdad de Oran* by Martín de Herrera (c. 1511), and *Historia partenopea* by Alonso Hernández (1512). Also part of this corpus are the *Vergel de nobles de los linajes de España* and the *Genealogía y blasón de los reyes de Castilla*, both by Pedro de Gracia Dei, and *Las siete edades del mundo* by Pablo de Santa María. All of these examples have in common a vagueness of purpose that remained an intractable theoretical problem well into the sixteenth century. This difficulty would extend to the writings on the New World.

It is within this broader context that poetry written after the discovery and conquest of the Americas should be read, because American-themed poems do not emerge from some literary vaccum, nor do they spontaneously appear from the minds of their creators. Rather, these poems are part of a rich literary tradition stemming from the encounter between chronicles in verse, medieval epic poetry and other poetic forms. One important point is that the reaction to the nature and inhabitants of the Americas made a profound impact on the poems and writings of the conquistadors, and it is during this moment of contact between tradition and innovation that American epic poetry is born. This overview explains the existence of the anonymous *Relación de la conquista y descubrimiento que hizo el Marqués don Francisco Piçarro en demanda de las provincias y rreynos que agora llamamos Nueva Castilla; dirigida al muy magnífico señor Juan Vázquez de Molina, secretario de la enperatriz y rreina, nuestra señora, y de su consejo* (c. 1538), an unfinished poem of 2,264 verses divided into two parts and composed of 283 octaves in *arte mayor*. The first part contains 209 octaves and the second 74, with each headed by an argument in prose that sums up the subsequent passage. It remains the poem with the richest description of Pizarro's three sea voyages on the eve of the conquest of Peru.

This poem is an example of the imitation and transformation of epic norms in the face of a new reality, as well as the appropriation of techniques borrowed from chronicles in verse and historical poems in a moment when the genre was waning. These literary occurrences coincide with the expansion of known geographical boundaries and create the possibility for the expression of a new reality. The aesthetic crisis transpiring in historiography in verse is overtaken by the pressing need for new forms of representation of American reality. It is in the midst of this crisis in representation that a dying genre gains new life, and undergoes a process of metamorphosis years after reaching the Renaissance epic had peaked.

The need to address the history of Spanish poetry, a subject in which many still have no background, is the theoretical aspect of greatest interest in *La conquista de Perú*. The topic of discovery and conquest of new American territories and its expression in traditional poetic forms (chronicles in verse and medieval epic), touch upon a central point in the relationship between literary and non-literary genres: between history and poetry, and importantly, the problem of "historical truth" in the poetic text. It is from one specific literary critique of epic poetry that we find the reformulated difference between history and poetry. In his commentary on Lucano's *Farsalia*, San Isidore distinguished between the *ordo naturalis* of history and the *ordo artificialis* of poetry (*Etymologiae*, VIII, vii, 10). San Isidore considers the difference between history and literature as thematic and not formal, and so in practice it is possible to use prose or verse interchangeably to write about historical topics (*Etymologiae*, I, 41). Nor did the medieval *artes poeticae* limit the use of metrics to deal with historical themes. In other words, historical matters can be written about in either prose or in verse. This is the tradition of historiography in verse to which Spanish chronicles in verse and historical poems belong. As Cátedra explains, because there was no "theoretical limit" the abandonment of rhyme by historians is an act born of the practice of writing coupled with the new circumstances of the time. This phenomenon perhaps "had its origin in the most ancient times when poetry and prose were not two radically separate forms of expression, but fell equally within the concept of 'discourse.' Poetry is speech reduced to meter." These common origins diverge over time, but even in the Middle Ages "discourse in verse and discourse in artistic prose were judged as interchangeable." The basis of these ideas come from several classical authors, including Quintilian, who believed that historiography "*proxima poeti et quodammodo carmen solutum*" (X, 1, 31). Given the importance of classical rhetoric and thanks to the transmission of his works from the Middle Ages to the time of Luis Vives (*De ratione dicendi*, 1532), it is possible to consider the ideas of Quintilian as the theoretical foundation for the confusion between history and poetry. It should be noted that Quintilian's ideas concerning the interchangeability between history and poetry were neglected by Aristotle, who established a difference between history and poetry based on the concept of verisimilitude in his *Poetics*.

The distinction between history and poetry, confused in thematic practice and marked by formal borrowings in some cases very difficult to isolate, is founded on the idea of truth, which implies the existence of a hidden truth only accessible to the "poet as bard, as seer, as theologian, as philosopher, as knower of all the sciences (including history)." Although these ideas can be traced back to classical Antiquity, it is during the Middle Ages that there is a resurgence of the debate on the essence of truth and its implications for poetry. This controversy has its basis in Christian theology—the ideas of St. Paul, St. Augustine and St. Thomas—and eventually extends to literature. Thus, Dante in *Convivio* mentions the existence of a concealed truth found within the meaning of the poem, and another truth accessible through the work's outward beauty. When explaining the differences between poetry and history in his *Genealogía de los dioses paganos*, Boccaccio refers to the works of Homer and Virgil and mentions the existence of something veiled which only reveals itself to the poet. From this moment on, literature introduces a secular vision of the truth which will coexist with a theological one.

As indicated by Guillermo Serés, this secular truth is essential in the development of the history of Spanish poetry, where it takes two divergent paths of interpretation. The first is a total defense of the secular version. The second is a rejection of any assertion of veracity in the poetic text, especially in the analyses of poetic texts, since critics view this claim as distorting divine truth as interpreted by Theology. The first position is represented by Enrique de Villena and the second by Alonso de Madrigal, el Tostado. The first stance chronicles the literary debate between Enrique de Villena and Fernán Pérez de Guzmán surrounding the interpretation of the *Aeneid*. Of their discussion in which Guzman defends the primacy of truth and Villena values more the adornment of words. Once again the epic appears in the examination of the relationship between history and literature. What is unique is that this analysis of the relationship between truth and epic poetry arises before the rediscovery of Aristotle's *Poetics*, thus pointing to arguments made by Quintilian on the close connection between history and poetry. Moreover, the ghost metaphor between truth and metric form used by Cátedra is doubly exemplary. First of all, it falls within an extensive list of authors who stress the spectral quality of the epic genre. Secondly, the quote indicates the extreme difficulty of this theoretical problem characterized by an indefinite formulation. This complexity is a pretext used by historians to abandon writing in verse, and at the same time, to support the form used in chronicles in verse. Authors will concentrate their desire to maintain fidelity to the truth at the expense of the genre's. Echoes of the debate between Villena and Pérez de Guzmán extend to the influence of Villena on the Marquis de Santillana, who incorporates the defense of a secular truth in poetry in his *Prohemio e carta*.

From 1492 onwards, the Conquest of the New World will transform the topic of truth in poetry so that now the problematic theme will be linked to the historical context of conquest-era ventures. From henceforth, the poetic form will be used to adorn depictions of the Conquest and will seek to enhance official Spanish campaigns both aesthetically and morally, thus fulfilling one of the genre's basic precepts. Ornamentation will play a crucial role in which the poem's organization and the exposition of the chosen theme, assuming an adherence to reality, will become subordinate to a temporal order similar to historial events. This purported image of historicity is a poetic technique long used in medieval Spanish literature. Over the years, the vacuum left by Spanish historians at the end of the fifteenth century was occupied by a new epic poetry that would gradually replace chronicle in verse. This transition period stretched from the end of the fifteenth century to the first part of the sixteenth century, and coincided with the historic moment of the discovery and conquest of the Americas. It is within this period that *La conquista del Perú* belongs. By mid-sixteenth century, new literary forms from Italy would give way to the Renaissance epic, which reappeared as an expansion of the neoaristotelian debate on ideas concerning the epic in the *Poetics*.

A careful reading of the Prologue of *La conquista del Perú* illuminates the relationship between history, truth and poetry by way of the work's treatment of historical events. Adopting the interrupted beginning technique (*in medias res*) in adherence to the norms of a direct style, the beginning of the poem saves unnecessary time spent creating a more pleasurable reading. The epic convention of the ellipsis also serves to suppress other historical aspects involving Pizarro's expedition that the author wants to conceal because they either threaten the image of Pizarro as hero or they introduce political or legal problems. Hence, the poem remains silent about the expedition of Pascual de Andagoya and about the agreements between those who laid the economic foundation of the expedition—Pizarro, Diego de Almagro and Hernado Luque.

*La conquista del Perú* does not rely only on the conventions of literary and historiographical models. The specific title (*Relación*) brings to mind legal rhetoric, considered the hegemonic discourse of the time because it was imposed on other forms of language devoted to the New World. In a rhetorical strategy that seeks greater attention and appreciation for the work, the use of the term *Relación* gives to the poem the authority of legal discourse aims to legitimize the content. To incorporate techniques of the relation into the poem, the author awards his work with an aspect of truth that goes beyond traditional historiographic formulas because he builds the text on the authority of legal discourse. We must remember that the letters of Columbus and Cortés helped to widely disseminate the rhetorical conventions of the relation and transform the genre into a prestigious form of writing, transcending the narrow influence of the notaries and even becoming subject to strict regulation by the Crown. Another result of the encounter with the New World, this change in mentality and in discursive models opened new horizons for the relation. From its newfound social prestige, the formula will be adopted by other literary genres such as poetry and the picaresque. One purpose stemming from the borrowing of characteristics of the relation was to support the claims of rights and privileges by slighted and forgotten conquistadors. Although it is likely that *La conquista del Perú* was written to provide legal support for other documents and evidence submitted by the conquistadors to counter divergent views put into circulation by enemies of Pizarro. *La conquista del Perú* highlights the importance and moral prestige associated with poetry at this early stage of the conquest. It also highlights the poem's heterogeneity, marked by borrowings from other discursive forms.

*La conquista del Perú* remains the first known epic poem chronicling the maritime expeditions of Francisco Pizarro from December 1524 until his encounter with Atahualpa in Cajamarca in November 1532, and is the text that offers the most detailed description of the conquistador's sea travels on the eve of the Andean conquest. A copy of a lost original, the manuscript of the poem—76 leaves—is at the National Library of Vienna. Johannn Andreas Sprecher de Bernegg prepared the first edition of the poem in 1848, F. Rand Morton the second in 1963, Adam Szászdi the third in 1981, Miguel Nieto the fourth in 1993, and Oscar Coello the most recent edition in 2001.

In order to make the work a Renaissance epic poem, Sprecher de Bernegg's edition alters the poem's original structure—283 octaves in arte mayor—and divides the first part into five cantos and the second part into three cantos. Bernegg also changes the title of the manuscript to *La conquista de la Nueva Castilla*. Each apocryphal canto is preceded by a brief summary of the argument expanded by Bernegg, while the stanzas are numbered and the spelling is modernized according to the criteria of the nineteenth century. This first edition includes historical annotations and tables of contents, the effect of which is to increase the confusion in the reader caused by presenting the work outside of its cultural context.

The edition of Rand Morton has the merit of restoring the text of the original manuscript, thus presenting the poem with its 283 stanzas divided into two parts. The first part ranges from octave I to CCIX and the second spans from octave CCX to CCLXXXIII, where the manuscript is interrupted. Morton devotes more attention to text than the poem's first editor, as the second edition contains few errors and none of these have an impact on the reading and interpretation of the text. Although Morton speaks of an anonymous author, he attributes the poem to Francisco de Xerez. One owes to Morton the reassessment of the poem's literary genre and a review of the classification of "chronicle in verse" established by Porras Barrenechea (*Los cronistas del Perú* 586). Despite these contributions, however, Morton incurs the same mistake as Bernegg. Both editors assign another title to the work, which creates confusion because of the lack of a uniform approach in defining the literary genre of text. As Amor y Vázquez noted in his review of Morton's book, this lack of classification is inconsistent because it refers to the work in various ways: "sixteenth century pre-Renaissance narrative poem with an American theme", "pre-Renaissance narrative poem," "pre-Renaissance epic" "heroic poem" and "historiographic essay" (483).

The edition of Adam Szászdi is preceded by a study that rejects Morton's argument that the author of the poem was Francisco de Xerez. Instead, Szászdi proposes a dual authorship of Alonso Brizeño and Diego de Silva. According to Szászdi, Brizeño was an eyewitness to the events, but was unable to write the foreword or the more literary fragments of the poem. Szászdi argues that these passages were written by Diego de Silva. In support of his theory, Szászdi refers to certain passages of the poem that denote a more elaborate literary style. However, he does clarify that Diego de Silva could not be the sole author of the work because he was not involved in Pizarro's expeditions from the beginning. In this edition, verses by Silva are reproduced in italics with the aim of establishing a difference with those of Brizeño. The result of Szászdi's thesis is the creation of a new text that differs from the original version of the manuscript because it allows for two distinct readings. According to Szászdi (129), Silva added 30 stanzas to the 180 stanzas of Part 1 of the original poem written by Brizeño, and 7 stanzas to the second part originally containing 67 stanzas.

The edition of Miguel Nieto modernizes the title of the book (*La conquista del Perú*) and establishes the text according to the manuscript of National Library of Vienna, checking variants against those found in the edition of Morton. Nieto's edition shows changes in the attribution of authorship, and thereby corrects Morton's assertion that the poem was authored by Francisco de Xerez. Based on a detailed analysis of the text, the editor dismisses the participation of Xerez in the composition of the poem not only because of discrepancies in style, but also the different ways of interpreting the events being narrated. In place of the names traditionally designated as authors of the poem, Nieto suggests returning to the idea of the anonymous author. Nieto's edition has 125 footnotes that combine philologic, historical, cultural, and scientific remarks. In this sense, Nieto follows the model used by Porras in his pioneering study of the first chronicles about the discovery and conquest of the Andes, and makes a comparative analysis of the historical aspects in the poem and their treatment in the histories and chronicles of the conquest of Peru.

The latest edition is by Oscar Coello, who collates the editions of Morton and Nieto, modernizing the accentuation of words and modifying the punctuation. He also takes into account a microfilm version of the manuscript that is located in the National Library of Lima. Coello's edition is preceded by an extensive study analyzing the manuscript's description, various editions, possible date of composition being between 1538 and 1539, and authorship by offering new considerations in favor of Diego de Silva as possible author. Among the most valuable contributions of this work is the section devoted to the influence of Juan de Mena's *El laberinto de fortuna*. This segment presents an intertextual analysis exploring the influence the medieval poet had on the American poem, especially in relation to the figures of fortune, the quest for fame and the intervention of providence. Based on studies by Navarro Tomás, Baehr, Belic and Foulché-Debolsc, Coello rigorously critiques the work's poetic form, and reevaluates its importance with more appropriate criteria. Coello's introduction concludes with an analysis of the general stylistic features, the most frequent rhetorical devices and the main actions of the poem. His analysis demonstrates that the author of *La conquista del Perú* knows and understands the poetic techniques of the time, thus overcoming the previous negative considerations concerning this poem (95-6).

The editors Morton, Szászdi, Nieto and Coello formulate their theories about the genre of the poem from the figure of fortune, which they represent in the following different ways: as personification (Morton), as structural element (Nieto) as feature of authorship (Szászdi) and as model for imitation (Coello). Moreover, as Coello clarifies: "The appreciation of the poem is enriched if we do not forget that the original meaning of the word *Fortuna* meant storm at sea" (74). Despite the various roles played by fortune in the work, all serve to sustain the editors' respective arguments surrounding the literary genre of the poem. There is no doubt that fortune has a privileged role in the text and that its model is Juan de Mena's *El laberinto de fortuna*, as Coello carefully analyzes, but there are a host of relevant aspects surrounding the influence of fortune. The repeated presence of fortune in the poem and in critical discourse highlights an important feature: patterns of repetition concerning this topic make it possible to suggest a close link between the poem and epic tradition. This relationship about the figure of fortune between *La conquista del Perú* and Mena's text links the poem to a literary work that is part of the tradition of the classical epic: the *Pharsalia* of Lucan. The origin of the connection between the two texts can be drawn in the following verse of the *Pharsalia* "Death is not subject to Fortune" (321), in which death prevails over fortune. Mena revises the idea of Lucan that death is more powerful than fortune, by arguing that death does not possess the power to defeat memory, which in turn subjects the individual to some specific circumstances imposed by fortune (Thomson 56). In this relationship, memory transcends death because it preserves the remembrance of lives and past actions. It is in this spirit that the anonymous poet's Foreward introduces the recalling of Pizarro's exploits for posterity as a function of poetry. This technique is according to the famous dictate that appears in *El laberinto de fortuna* which states that the obligation of poetry is to preserve heroes' exploits (Mena 66).

The Foreword of *La conquista del Perú* frames the work and contains summaries of the author's main ideas and principle literary topics. The section uses dedicatory rhetoric and highlights the manipulation of truth to present an idealized image of Pizarro that corresponds to the ideals of chivalry. The technique of *ordo artificialis* organizes the text from an immediate present, in contrast to the traditional method of classical and medieval epic poetry, which preferred to deal with matters from a distant point in time. In this sense *La conquista del Peru* follows the rule of temporal proximity, begun by Lucan's *Pharsalia*, and employed by fifteenth-century chronicles in verse. This new way of poetically representing reality is another transformation of the genre and breaks with those epic traditions based on the idealized model of Virgil's *Aeneid*. Perhaps due to this conscious break with traditional models there is a conflict with another topic, that of pressing urgency. Thus, an urgent call for attention reinforces immediacy in the poem.

The style of the Foreword's opening lines announces the need for recounting Pizarro's actions as occurring during an epoch in crisis. This first moment of doubt and insecurity of the present characterizes the opening sentence and creates the first image of the text, which will later link to the stanzas of the first verse. This depiction is also related to the other objective of metaphorically uniting the chaotic present with a past moment of calm and tranquility. It is based on this image that a conflict is established between a distant, unchanged past and a nostalgic feeling due to the sense of an irreparable loss, one of the main topics of Spanish poetry following Jorge Manrique's work. The mastery of the Prologue, which anticipates the same technique used in the poem, consists of creating a new space of hope that moves forward toward new possibilities and creates a second chance for those who possessed a chivalresque notion of adventure. It is from this context that the image of the New World appears as a new physical and moral frontier that must be conquered, overcoming the declining of the chronicle in verse. This new poetry emerges from the search for novel stories to tell and is an example of a renewal of the epic genre.

In the initial line of the Prologue, that which links past, present and future are the themes of knightly virtue, old values, possibilities created in New World territories, and the temporal space of present and future. These three chronological moments converge in the person of Francisco Pizarro, who is depicted in three courtly ways alluding to three different moments in time: Don, governor and Marquis. These three historically successive portrayals appear simultaneously in the text with conventions of poetic fiction. The title of the poem and the Prologue concentrate on Pizarro as Marquis, while the summary of the first part focuses on his role as governor. Within the poem he is called captain because this was his only title when he undertook the expedition in 1524. He obtained the status of governor in 1529, during his trip to Spain (a journey that is not mentioned neither in the Foreword, nor in the poem), and the title of Marquis was granted in 1537. It is true that the title of the poem and the

Prologue must have been written after the poem itself, and that their content was perhaps updated, but the importance of noble titles is a way to infuse in the poem a symbolic force of authority, and consequently more semblance of truth to the readers of the court.

It is my assertion that the passage about Pizarro's titles demonstrates the conventions of poetic fiction in the face of historical truth. That is, if the poet is completely committed to following historical reality, then his perspective would be very limited and would promptly expose every detail of the daily events which happened to Pizarro during his expedition years. This coincides with the function of the chronicle or historical relation, but not of the epic. The possibilities offered by poetic fiction are to give the author the opportunity to change the real world within the poem, and to create a poetic truth, namely, a new type of convention that has a life of its own without breaking with reality. One of the most interesting aspects of the poem is the adoption of the formula of treatments and courtesies, a highly respected practice at the time. The author addresses this difficulty by respecting chronological order within the work, and using the Foreword (following the conventions of the same rhetoric), to depict the true level of Pizarro's social position. As a text preceding the poem, the Foreword also prepares the reader and influences his morale, because the adventures being read are not those of a simple captain lost in the South Sea, but rather the exploits of powerful noble who ultimately acquires the title of Marquis.

One consequence of this passage is that it reveals fundamental differences between the poem and the chronicle, a genre marked by a faithful detailing of actions and an adherence to chronology. *La conquista del Perú* uses the techniques of ellipsis and the magnification of Pizarro's expeditions to such an extent that it is necessary to modify the inner world of the poem, though never going beyond those parameters defined by the *res gestae*. There is never a mention neither in the Foreword nor in the poem of magical or supernatural elements; moreover, writing follows an *ordo artificialis* in which there is no strict chronological order of events. The poem is characterized by an artistic re-elaboration, as in the concurrent mention of Pizarro's titles and the absence of the conquistador's trip to Spain in 1529. Historical truth is transformed according to poetic conventions because it presents a richer simultaneity (1524, 1529, 1537), which thus allows the reader to simultaneously observe Pizarro's origins and social ascent.

Another way that the Prologue announces is to warn against not knowing of Pizarro's actions,—"podrían careçer de tal conoçimiento"—a technique following the long tradition of "he who possess knowledge should divulge it" and which serves as an imperative that the poet must fulfill. Any questioning of the true aim of writing this poem is therefore rhetorically justified. The anonymous author goes on to explain the reasons for the dedication to the Secretary Juan Vázquez de Molina, and produces two short examples to support his argument. In the first, he uses the metaphor of jewels, a strategy which compares the profession of the poet with that of a jeweler. In this medieval vision of poetry as artifice, the result is one in which the poet possesses the perfection of a goldsmith's skills and abilities. In the second example, the poet presents a complicated conceptual construct around the popular medieval metaphor of the mirror, through which the idea of poetry is conceived of as a shared act of creation. This is possibly adopting the technique of false modesty, by way of belittling. It is furthermore true that the passage utilizes the praise of rulers strategy, which, coupled with false modesty, appears to achieve *captatio benevolentiae*. These multiple techniques create a conceptual game through the metaphor of sunlight and the mirror, where the secretary Vázquez de Molina appears as a central figure. Beyond the rhetorical devices mentioned, the metaphor of gold alludes to the Peruvian riches that Pizarro possesses and may give to those who support his political aspirations in the Court. The statement seeking support from a major political authority refers to the presence of historical truth which, according to the conventions of poetry, appears hidden amongst metaphors.

Fulfilling its required role, the Foreword offers the reasons for Pizarro to remain faithful to his goals in times of adversity, and summarizes Pizarro's view of life as one of the King's subjects. This recalls the ideals of a medieval vassal able to cope with danger because his actions are motivated by an ethics of service to the King. This passage is the most important in the Prologue because the author describes the relationship between history and poetry, understood as a process in which historical truth can come to be known thanks to the activity of the poets ("este metro"). This section also draws attention to the predominance of the act of discovery on the eve of the Conquest, not only by the logic of discourse (following the requirements of an *ordo naturalis*, but rather by an open contradiction with the wording of the title that favors the element of conquest over discovery. In an allusion to the norms of chivalry, the final part of the Prologue ends requesting that the secretary Vázquez de Molina serve as patron to support the poem. The last part of this fragment of the Prologue is a statement on the poetic ideals of the author, which highlights knowledge of the technique of preserving the memory of the past. Following the model of Juan de Mena in the *El laberinto de fortuna,* the anonymous author's central idea is preserving the past. The need to remember the previous heroic deeds through poetry, namely poetry with the aim of maintaining historical memory, becomes apparent from the following obligatory Menesque reference. Fernán Pérez de Guzmán expresses a similar sentiment in his *Loores de los claros varones de España* when he regrets past heroic deeds forgotten due to the lack of their being immortalized by poets. This is the context of literary history to which the Prologue alludes when it mentions that the deeds of Pizarro may be in danger of being forgotten. Thus, by adopting a narrative style in the Preface, the author can explain the circumstances of composition of the work.

The poem begins by mentioning the departure date of the expedition of Francisco Pizarro. The poet resorts to the standard order for chronicles and historical stories because he accurately quotes the date of departure of the expedition (Lara Garrido 37). The fact that this temporal reference is the only one that appears in this section devoted to the first trip allows the coordinates of space to be established from the temporal references, according to the use of the religious calendar to name discovered territories. Place names in the poem are linked to important dates of the Christian calendar following an ancient mariner custom (Martínez-Valverde 151-70; Romero 1-23). For example, with the phrase "on the feast day of St. Luçía" the author notes that the departure occurred on December 13, 1524, that is, during the same year that all the planets were aligned with Pisces,—February 24, 1524. This year resulted in a trail of apocalyptic predictions about the deluge, as can be read in many books on the subject have appeared on that date in Europe (Díaz Jimeno 55-68). There is a need to clarify that the closeness of the dates of the aligning of planets and the issuance of Pizarro should be seen as a mere coincidence, since the latter came six months after the astronomical phenomenon; therefore, its role in the composition and references of the poem are relative. I only stress this point because previous readings overlooked the fact that the continued references to good fortune respond to a time dominated by fear and insecurity in Europe. These references may also be present in *La conquista del Perú*. The most important aspect of fortune in work is the role of imitation of major literary models, which includes the *Laberinto de fortuna* by Juan de Mena, as Coello evidenced in a detailed study of intertextuality in the Peruvian poem (51-136).

The date establishes the extent of the interrupted start by omitting the reference to any previous event and thus avoiding mention of Pizarro's life prior to the expedition. The omission of biographical information not only responds to the rhetorical strategy of excluding unnecessary details, but also the aesthetization of reality through the use of embellished poetic discourse (Quint 3). The initial image of the poem depicts Pizarro at his departure,—"Don Françisco Piçarro del Puerto salía" (139)—and associates his name with the metaphor of the ship, thus infusing traditional poetic elements into the heroic character of the conquistador. It draws attention to the way in which the poem deletes other aspects of the expedition, including the agreement between Pizarro, Almagro, and the governor Pedrarias de Avila as it appears in the *Relación de los primeros descubrimientos de Francisco Pizarro y Diego de Almagro* (Salas 49). Because the most important aspect of the poem is the triumph of Pizarro over fortune, this deletion of aspects of reality in the poem follows a binary structure as necessitated by an imitation of the theme of fortune as depicted by Mena (Coello 70). The technique of combining aspects of reality and poetry allows for the manipulation of historical truth for the sake of poetic beauty. This notion is observed with the "falta de prósperos vientos," a traditional poetic strategy used to highlight the difficult departure due to the delay caused by the high winds. Anticipating the difficulties that await the travelers while also constituting an allegory about the challenge every poet faces at the outset of creating a work, this example imitates the model of *The Argonauts*.

Due to its rhetorical meaning, the idea of navigation in *La conquista del Perú* is of great significance since the idea of the trip in the poem has two meanings: material and discursive (Hartog 8). In the text there are two journeys:

the expedition of Francisco Pizarro and the imaginary journey of the poet that begins when he gives an account of the adventures of the conqueror. Travel in the work presents two epistemological problems, however: on one hand, Pizarro's challenge is the physical discovery of Peru, and on the other hand, the dilemma facing the anonymous author is how to represent sea travel poetically since that way of representation had no precedent in traditional Spanish literature. Faced with this problem, the poet turns to the best-known classical examples of Homer and Virgil, two authors that used their characters Ulysses and Aeneas to deal with the relationship between travel and knowledge. In other words, hermeneutical ability generated within the travel from each displacement originates from the learning of new information. The poet narrates the maritime expedition of Pizarro, and also alludes to a metaphorical voyage, so the sea additionally represents language and the poetic imagination as an infinite horizon or unlimited expanse. This metaphor of the nautical journey is especially useful in describing stages of transition; their use in the poem relates to the epistemological role indicated in relation to the classical epic (Dougherty 4-5), although it should be stated that the classical tradition of travel as source of knowledge transcends epic poems, including texts belonging to other forms of language, among which are the works of Herodotus, Pliny, and Strabo (Romm 200-18). The poet utilizes the travel metaphor and other spatial metaphors because they are the most appropriate way of figuratively representing the challenges and difficulties of Pizarro's expedition, while at the same time transforming the epic genre through the writing of a new topic.

Pizarro's willingness to suffer hardships in order to achieve his objective corresponds to the theme of heroic constancy in the mercurial face of fortune. This vision of fortune comes from *El laberinto de fortuna* (Coello 77) and is embodied in the following verses: "presuma de vos y de mí la Fortuna/non que nos fuerça, mas que la forçamos" (Mena 137). Because *La conquista del Perú* chronicles a journey of conquest, i.e. an image of expansion into unknown spaces, the expedition route is the linchpin of the argument, giving the word "vía" the metaphorical function noted by Northrop Frye (212). It is from this rhetorical trip that metaphors are defined according to the argument posed in the *Poetics* of Aristotle, in which the idea of displacement is best represented through metaphor and the *Odyssey*-inspired image of the anchored ship (¶ 1457b). The ship has since been metaphorized in Greco-Latin rhetoric, where similar literary examples appear. The significance of this image in classical tradition compels Curtius to consider it a specific trope: the nautical metaphor. The critic draws attention to the seeming insignificance of this symbol when he clarifies that this trope actually represented the creative process. In Ovid and Virgil, composition of a work is compared to a voyage by sea (Curtius 189-90). The figurative use of nautical imagery allows readers to see the close link between poetic authority and tradition, as it appears in works by Hesiod, Pindar and other Greek poets (Dougherty 20). That technique was taken up by Ennio, Virgil, Horace and Ovid in Latin poetry, so that navigation becomes a key topic in the history of poetry. The symbolism of the sea in constant motion recalls the

Aristotelian definitions of the metaphor: transportation, translation, and transfer (*Rhetorics* ¶ 1405th, 1405b ¶ ¶ 1407th, 1412nd ¶ ¶ 1413rd; *Poetics* ¶ 1457b). *La conquista del Perú* is organized around one unifying metaphor: the nautical journey. Navigation in the beginning of the poem, however, is the center of the story because of its empirical reference, that is to say, the historical facts of Pizarro's first expedition in 1524 become the backbone of language as a fiction, namely as a metaphor of the journey. In the poem the nautical metaphor acquires two senses: the literal, which refers to the experience of traveling and links it with tales of travel, and the figurative, which alludes to creation as a voyage in which many obstacles must be overcome to finish the work.

In the departure scene, the author uses the allusion to the "travajos" of the travelers in order to present the reason for the difficulty and danger characteristic to all navigation. "Travajos" appears to be a Latinism utilized in the sense of suffering since it is common in the literary language of the time. The poet also insists in the idea of danger by referring to it when Pizarro leaves land to set sail: "se mete en la mar, dexando la tierra" (139). This quote marks the passage from land to sea, perhaps a medieval vestige of the trope of fear of the sea (Zumthor 169). In a poem dedicated to navigation beyond the known limits of the South Sea, this theme appears hinted at when the anonymous author discusses leaving the mainland to begin travel on sea. Fear of the sea is coupled with the idea of human inferiority before life's adversities, and appears nuanced by Christian ideas, in particular the appeal to providence as a safeguard for fortune; this corresponds to themes found in *El laberinto de fortuna* by Juan de Mena—(Coello 85). The allusion to the fear of navigating is a subject of extensive poetic genealogy, among which includes *The Argonauts* of Apollonius of Rhodes. It is precisely in this work where the fear of navigation on the Black Sea, the dreaded rocks in the Sea (Apollonius 99), models epic poems. In this regard, the *Pharsalia* contains verses which refer to the navigations of Jason and the Argonauts as a transgressive act that violates the natural limits of land imposed on man, (Lucan 146), an idea that can also stem from the idea of navigation as a condemnable act that appears in Sextus Propertius and in classical Greek authors. The closest model is the *El laberinto de fortuna*: "Para quien teme la furia del mar/ e las tempestades reçela de aquélla, el mejor reparo es no entrar en ella,/perder la cobdiçia del buen navegar;" (121). Behind this idea of fear of the sea is the other aspect of the metaphor of the ship, and its ambivalent character due to the fact that it also symbolizes death. In this regard, the metaphor appears in the *Aeneid* (VI, 295-304) through the example of the boat of Caron (Tola 48). This funeral element of navigation and its dangers remains exposed in the discussions between Pizarro and his crew. The author allegorizes the two positions of the poets surrounding the theme of navigation. These two positions appear in the poem in debate form, exemplified by the dialogue between the voices of the crew and Pizarro: a multiple and anonymous voice that insists on returning to Spain and leaving the company counters the voice of Pizarro, which defends the need to continue the journey. The alternating voices in the poem creates "an itinerary defined by recurring points of contradiction" (Conley 251) that appears in every part of the territory where the debate occurs between sailors and Pizarro. The dispute between voyagers takes on a discursive dimension because these dialogues also create a space where the poem unfolds: the poetic space. The conflict between continuing on or returning is born out of moments of pain, hunger and death that appear at certain intervals in the poem because they are based on the itinerary of navigation and enhance the poem's size. In this passage the poem alters the topic of fear of the sea in order to establish a contrast between earthly places as a source of danger, and the sea as the route to salvation. This produces a reversal of the usual depiction of the earth as a giver of life, developed from *Works and Days* by Hesiod. The travelers prefer the sea to land, and their collective cry evokes the frightening image of no return as an allegory of death in the sense that it appears in the *Iliad* (Pucci 128) and perhaps also alludes to the famous image of the winged vessels as allegory of death in the *Odyssey* (XI 125). Hence, we observe the insistence of the expedition members to embark on and return to Panama, though Pizarro manipulates in his rallying speeches the fact that only from the sea can the voyagers continue their voyage on and search for new territories. Through the debate scene, the poet recreates the two possibilities for travel poetry: the one-directional journey, without return, and the roundtrip, corresponding to the classical models of Ulysses and Aeneas (Hartog 18). The expedition members have a desire to return, while Pizarro represents a heroic will and does not consider return, but rather the continuance of the quest to reach the goal of discovery. The dispute between Pizarro and crew is a major trope in the poem since it also helps to organize and establish the boundaries of poetic discourse. The section of the first journey ends with a temporary return to the vicinity of Panama, and though at the end of the second trip Pizarro moved to Spain in 1529 to solicit support in court, this trip to Spain is absent since the poem only narrates the American adventures of Pizarro. In this aspect *La conquista del Perú* corresponds to the *Relación de los primeros descubrimientos de Francisco Pizarro y Diego de Almagro,* a text that recounts the actions of the first two trips, but makes no mention of the efforts of Pizarro in Spain.

Pizarro always considers past experience to negotiate with the crew, sometimes seeming to agree to yield to their demands, as when he sends Montenegro to the Island of Pearls to search for food, or during the harangue before the first battle that recalls his experiences in Caribana. In these scenes the poem appeals to the literary tradition that establishes an association between the figurative use of navigation images and poetic authority (Dougherty 20), because Pizarro always succeeds at continuing on with the navigation and with the campaign. Similarly, the poet can continue writing his work because navigation appears as a prefiguration of the poetic process. The character of Pizarro may be modeled on the figure of tenacity, which responds to the topic of *Polutlas*, symbolized by Ulysses in the classical poetic tradition (Hartog 16), and embodies the theme of the epic's ability to direct the end of the poem, because he is capable of maintaining the course, similar to the image that appears in contemporary emblem books like the *Symbolicae Quaestiones* by

Achille Bocchi (Bologna 1555) in which the captain of the ship maintained firm control over the crew and the course of navigation (Thomson 26). In *La conquista del Perú*, the notion of the search contains more than one possible meaning, because it is a quest for new territories, markets and products and coincides with Columbian rhetoric as analyzed by Zamora (17-19). Unlike Columbian discourse that offers words for gold, however, the Pizarrian poem does not mention the ownership of gold and riches garnered since the first encounter with Amerindians. The existence of such spoils was recorded by the testimony of other contemporary chronicles, such as the *Relación de los primeros descubrimientos de Francisco Pizarro y Diego de Almagro*, a testimony of the first two trips, *La conquista del Perú, llamada la Nueva Castilla* by an anonymous author that appears in Seville in 1534 and reported the actions of third trip Pizarro from 1531 to 1533, and the *Verdadera relación de la conquista del Perú y provincia del Cuzco, llamada la Nueva Castilla* by Francisco de Xerez, published in Seville in 1534 and considered the most detailed testimony from the original texts about the conquest of Peru (Salas 37-251). The omission of material from Pizarro's cargo ship seeks to conceal the economic objective of the expedition and is one of the points in the poem that reveals the problematic relationship between truth and poetry expressed in an undefined way. Gold and economic benefits were not mentioned in the poem, but rather existed in the historical reality since the first voyage of Pizarro in 1524. The resources assuring the continuation of the conquistador's mission are precisely the gold and riches obtained from this initial voyage; in particular, the riches garnered during the second expedition are those which enabled Francisco Pizarro to visit Spain in 1529 and achieve the *Capitulación de Toledo* agreement that gave him full powers over unconquered Peruvian territory (Varón 63-86).

The author of *La conquista del Perú* adopts a rhythm that transcends territory in a dynamic that goes from the known to the unknown and that, together with the elements of adventure, denotes, identifies and defines space. This development projects into the unknown and in this sense is also an adventure. The idea of the quest reinforces the ship metaphor as highlighting the uncertainty that marks the departure from a known and safe place: Panama. This indicates the beginning of the route and of the poem from a point in geographic space that functions as a territorial border and also serves as a framework that organizes poetic space since the poem is written from Panama to Panama. The text establishes the limits from Panama, which operates as the only hope in the face of distress and failure, and as a toponomy of what is known, of what is certain and of what is life. An indicator of salvation in the eyes of the mariner, the notion of the border is a reference point inscribed on the map and in the memory. The poem begins from Panama and develops around the promise of returning to Panama. This return is always delayed at Pizarro's behest, a technique modeled after Columbus's example of negotiating with his crew to prevent a riot. The fruitless search for Peruvian territory culminates this first expedition with the momentary interruption of returning to Panama, showing a vision of territory as an unstable space since Pizarro and his troops have to withdraw after the battle at the Puerto de las Piedras, return to Chuchama and then recover the "lost" territory. Since space is not conquered militarily and indeterminate points along the coast still cannot be precisely defined within the text, the poem's first part describes space as being undefined and mysterious.

The idea of the ship traveling into the unknown is the image that organizes the work as a poem about navigation, travel and discovery. The image also gives the text its qualities of movement and change that come from the challenge of writing about a subject without any major Spanish literary tradition. It is important to remember that in 1538, the year surrounding the work's composition, there were no epic poems about Christopher Columbus or Hernan Cortés that could have served as models for *La conquista del Perú*. The difficulty presented by the absence of a literary tradition is ressolved by using the travel log and other documents about Pizarro's expedition as the inspiration for the story; hence the poem can be read as a travel narrative. This discursive mode that supports the poem establishes textual limits, namely, the descriptive space that is conditioned by the geographical scope. The innovative feature of the poem is that space becomes the core of the composition, creating a new space in the history of poetry. The image of navigation that begins as a generic event now defines itself as an action within a given space: the coast of the South Sea. Faced with an intial verse depicting offshore navigation, the poem confines the journey to the coast and its environs, thus echoing Eufemo's classical suggestion in *The Argonauts* of staying within the vicinity of the coast (Apollonius 228). This journey along the coast is a curious deviation from historical reality, because Pascual de Andagoya had advised Pizarro to sail offshore to avoid strong coastal winds.

The importance of the voyage by sea in Pizarro's expedition is highlighted even more given the fact that among the few documents which feature this trip, appear the oldest cartographic testimonies of South American West coast—the navigation letter of Bartolome Ruiz and Fernan Perez of Peñate 1527, and the map of Diego Ribero of 1529. If these documents have suvived to modern times, it is very likely that the author of *La conquista del Perú* had access to them, along with lost travel logs. The dependence that the poem has on these documents is reflected in the structure of *La conquista del Perú*, which can be read as an itinerary that traces the route of Pizarro's ships to their final destination, serving as a guide for the way in which this imaginary trip figuratively delineates the coast through a toponymy which supplements and interprets maps and logs for the expedition. To understand the importance of this poem, it is necessary to remember that, unlike the expeditions of Christopher Columbus and Hernán Cortés, there is no logbook or letter about the discovery of Peru. The poem is one of the few known testimonies on the first expedition of Pizarro. In that sense, the work assumes the role of poetic letter of discovery and presents the reader with a geographical vision of the New World through a description of the coastal route of Northwest South America. The only other comparison would be found in the details of the *Relación de los primeros descubrimientos de Francisco Pizarro y Diego de Almagro,* which also mentions the people and places encountered during Pizarro's first trip (Salas 49 - 63).

The poem outlines the route of the epic genre in the New World and establishes linkages between the cosmographical and topographical dimensions described in the chronicles of the Indies. Therefore, it is not a map, but rather an itinerary whose cognitive function is different because it is not a full recount and does not purport to be an exhaustive description of the territory. Omitting several aspects of the expedition and the biography of Pizarro, the itinerary is an open guide to the imagination. The text creates a poetic space which produces in the reader a feeling of simultaneously being in and out of place (Conley 243). For example, place names in the poem act as physical limits to identify points along the route and thus the space described in the text takes on a geographical position while also recreating in the imagination of readers these unknown locations following the literary tradition. *La conquista del Perú* insists on the mention of New World territory, and it is precisely this point which moves the representation of individuals living within the geographical space to a secondary role. References to indigenous populations in this section of the poem are very rare, forming part of the background in relation to the land. The poet emphasizes a physical and psychological aloofness that maintains distant contact with the Amerindians. From that detached perspective, he names the land through toponymy. He is not able to denote other specific aspects of indigenous life nor can he provide an ethnographic reading of the Amerindian societies he encounters. Opposed to this distant gaze is the presentation of Francisco Pizarro. The poetic voice presents the conquistador as an idealized epic hero in harmony with the objectives of the expedition.

Much of the poetic space is created from the description of the land, but it is the literary tradition that provides the strategies to represent geographical space. Among those literary methods are formulaic techniques, metaphor and imaginary which develop a new poetic language. A rhythm arises which alternates between movement and disruption, and the structure of the poem reflects the detailing of the navigation. The discursive space of the text is distinguished by a narrative and descriptive register. Rather than providing a discussion of the specific lands of an indigenous group, the poem mentions a indefinite territory called "Peru," and additionally records the names given to certain coastal locales in order to take possession of the territory. Since the poem describes geographical space based on stories and myths that had traveled to Panama, Peruvian territory remains a kind of amorphous space because actual physical limits were unknown (Busto 11-23). In this vision of Peru the auditory over the visual dominates, because it is precisely the mystery surrounding the unknown name which creates a seductive draw for the conquerors, who associate the name of Peru with a mythical land of fabulous wealth. This land offers unlimited possibilities for the poetic imagination, and the geographical space that is described in the text appears discontinuous with topographical names corresponding to an indefinite image. In this vision of the geography of

Peru, named places emerge as a virtual space, surrounded by the vastness of the sea and unknown lands that extend beyond the coast into a vast abyss.

In *La conquista del Perú,* poetic space is represented along the lines of the Portulano map, which, due to chronological and mnemotechnic reasons, presents the description of the coastline based on a strict denomination of places. In contrast with other epic poems, *La conquista del Perú* lacks mythological allusions and interventions by religious figures. There are several reasons for these omissions, including the influence of the Portulan map in the composition of the work, given the preference of the Portulan map for descriptive elements. Zumthor clarifies that the Portulan map "is not only a register of places; it perceives and represents some intervals: distances" (316-17). These intervals are depicted in the text as imaginative spaces where the voice of the author creates a poetic milieu. Reading these moments in the section devoted to Pizarro's initial voyage helps in the understanding of the relationship between physical and poetic space. In this first part, the description of the land is subordinate to poetic space, but in the sections dedicated to the second and third trips, the descriptions of the physical space are more extensive, even chronicling a lengthy tour through the Andean landscape during the last trip. Moreover, the names mentioned in the poem—Puerto de Piñas, Puerto Deseado, Puerto de Hambre, Puerto de la Candelaria and Puerto de Piedras—adhere to the mnemonic device of the Portulan map and lack a symbolic meaning. Following the literary tradition in which the dis-covery is understood as a "visual revelation ", the description of points on the poetic itinerary dominates the land through a language that appoints and assigns the new territories with a name (Zumthor 231). This topic of poetic unveiling (Serés 153-59) is present in *La conquista del Perú* where the anonymous poet makes readers see places that were previously unknown through imagination. Upon narrating the adventures of Pizarro's expedition, the author depicts the lands and transforms them into familiar places. Thus, poetry recreates these worlds through a language developed through rhetorical devices. Space is metaphorized within the text following a "territorialization" of language, which appoints in order to exist, and which in turn "occupies, defines, and defends" (Zumthor 366). The poem mimics the allegory of a sea voyage which functions as a novel rhetorical mechanism that is linked to new areas of reality, and ultimately seeks to enrich the language. Resulting in moments of expansion of language within the poem, the metaphor of travel allows for the naming of new spaces in addition to those already known. In this sense, *La conquista del Perú* plays a pragmatic role similar to that of other texts such as the letter Pedrarias Dávila (April 1525), the *Relación de los primeros descubrimientos de Francisco Pizarro y Diego de Almagro,* letters of Espinosa and Antonio de la Gama, the relation of Pascual de Andagoya, the anonymous chronicle *La conquista del Perú, llamada la Nueva Castilla* (Seville 1534), or the *Verdadera relación de la conquista del Perú y provincia del Cuzco, llamada la Nueva Castilla* by Francisco de Xerez, published in Seville in 1534 (Porras, *Las relaciones primitivas* 38-68; 79-102), because the main objective of the *La conquista del Perú* is not to interpret the conquest, but to legitimize it through writing, though its evocative power is more intense because it is linked to feelings and emotional memory firmly rooted in the collective imagination through the poetic tradition that originates in the *chansons de geste* and the frontier epic. This power to evoke is another manifestation of poetic space. It results in a territory that is located in another dimension, namely a "there," or an "elsewhere" (Zumthor 361). By their remoteness and inaccessibility, the new lands represent this space, as conquerors were not able to reach the Peruvian territory in the first trip of 1524, but in the two successive trips ending in 1531. In other words, it is a representation of poetic space that there is an otherworldly presence that is always elsewhere. Poetry serves as a vehicle of expression by way of language because it is under the pretext of telling a story that follows the route of the expedition Pizarro that the poem is actually being written. This quality creates a narration of the discovery and appears as a virtual entity because the end of the story about the discovery of Peru is always delayed for another time, thereby prolonging the reading of the poem. Moreover, the postponement of the representation of physical space is due to the fact that the Peruvian territory is subject to a fruitless search that will culminate in a return to Panama. This event is a momentary interruption, showing a vision of the territory as an indefinite area, because Peru had not yet been conquered militarily and could not be defined precisely in the text. Unable to overtake the American landscape, Pizarro decides to embark on a return to the environs of Panama. The irony apparent in the poem is that, in order to continue on with the expedition, the conqueror must return to his point of origin and thereby begin a journey similar to that of an epic hero (Nieto, "Discovery" 95). The poem also modifies this return since it blends the end of the first trip with the start of the second, thus transforming historical truth through the adornment of poetry.

*La conquista del Perú* is not just one of the first poetic testimonies of the discovery and conquest of the Americas, but is also the discovery of a new poetic form: the American epic poem. Within this imaginary state the poet is also able to mentally explore and thus achieve an intellectual discovery: the writing of the first poem about the conquest of the Americas. Unable to separate history from poetry in his work, especially in the portions on navigation, the anonymous poet is a discoverer of new territories. This unlimited imaginative space is the place of poetry. It creates the opportunity for the author to write for the first time about the expedition of Francisco Pizarro, and so the topic offers unlimited possibilities for the discovery of new poetic territories.

# CHAPTER 3

## Epic, Haunting, and Violence in *Los actos y hazañas valerosas del capitán Diego Hernández de Serpa* (1564) by Pedro de la Cadena

The study of the colonial epic is distinguished by a number of myths, among which is the foundational myth that situates the origins of American epic poetry in *La Araucana* by Alonso de Ercilla (Part 1, 1569), leaving aside those poems that were written before. In his book *La poesía épica del siglo de oro*, Frank Pierce gives a periodization of the epic beginning from the *Christo Pathia* by Juan de Quirós (1552), and also summarizes the critical history of the genre starting from the *Arte poética en romance castellano* by Miguel Sánchez de Lima (1580). However, it is imperative to keep in mind that there are also earlier written poems and other treaties. This critical silence is the cause of the exclusion of the literary work *Los actos y hazañas valerosas del capitán Diego Hernández de Serpa* (1564) by Pedro de la Cadena, a short epic about the conquest of Venezuela, and without which it is impossible to understand the evolution and development of the epic poem in Latin America.

The literary models are the Spanish rhymed chronicles of the late fourteenth century. This heroic narrative poetry, known as the "new epic", differs in several important aspects from the medieval epic that preceded it, including the use of the *copla de arte mayor* in response to the *cuaderna vía,* and the inclusion of recent history rather than remote past events (Vaquero 45-63). One of the most prominent examples of this type of work is the *Poema de Alfonso XI* of Rodrigo Yáñez, composed in 1348 and a rhyming chronicle that celebrates the reconquest of a historic building. Another representative work of this new epic is *Consolatoria de Castilla* by Juan Barba (1487), a poem in praise of the Catholic Monarchs. This "history in verse" encompasses both chronicles and rhymed poems, highlighting the permeability of genres. Among this innovative form of poetry are works such as the *Panegírico en alabanza de la reyna Isabel* by Diego Guillén de Avila (1499), *Vida rimada de Fernán González* (ca. 1498) by Gonzalo de Arredondo, *Ystorias de la divinal victoria y nueva adquisición de la muy insigne ciudad de Orán* by Martín de Herrera (1511), *Historia Partenopea* by Alonso Hernández (1512), and *Práctica de las virtudes de los buenos reyes d'España* by Francisco de Castilla (1517), among others (Cátedra 1-25). It is precisely within this broad context that we should examine the production of poetry written after the conquest of America, because American epic poems do not emerge from a historical vacuum. These compositions belong to a culture that originates from contact between rhymed chronicles, the medieval epic and other poetic forms. It is also important to note that the reaction to nature and the inhabitants of the Americas left a deep imprint on the poems and narratives of the conquerors, and as a direct result of this exchange between tradition and novelty, authors began to write the new American epic poetry. This epic production helps in understanding the historical and cultural context of *Los actos y hazañas valerosas del capitán Diego Hernández de Serpa* by Pedro de la Cadena, an epic poem of 1, 051 verses written in *"endecasílabos* without rhyme"(Tejedor 183 ).

The manuscript of the poem is inserted inside a volume in the Library of El Escorial (Diij-25, pages 221-246). In 1913 Marcelino Menéndez Pelayo was the first who mentioned the existence of it in the *History of Latin American poetry*, however, his comments on this work were negative: "consider[ed] written in loose verse or in rather vile prose "(68). This critical reception seems to have influenced the lack of subsequent editions and studies on the work. The first edition of the poem appeared in 1973, in *El primer poema de tema venezolano*, by Pablo Ojer and Efraín Subero. The aim of both authors is to publicize the text of Pedro de la Cadena and assess its importance in the literature of colonial Venezuela. The edition is accompanied by two studies. In "Historical aspects of the first poem on Venezuela," Pablo Ojer discusses the historical and geographical context of the work, the controversy surrounding the importance of the poem, and the life of the author and the protagonist. It also examines the question of the historicity of Act VI on the attack against the Ingenios and Act VII dedicated to the war against the Caribs. The second essay, "Literary Aspects of the first poem of Venezuela" by Efrain Subero, examines the landscape of aboriginal and black folk literature in Venezuela, as well as analyzes the poem's location in time and space, structure, style and main subjects to conclude with a critical assessment of the poem. This work is accompanied by seven appendices on the formation process of Venezuelan nationality and testimony from colonial chronicles, travelers, linguists, indigenous, African and folk literature. The Edition by Ojer and Subero has the merit of rescuing from oblivion the poem, establishing a first edition from a historical and philological study of the text, and providing a comparative analysis between the text and critical comments. The issue also features a spelling modernization that clarifies obscure passages of the manuscript.

Pedro de la Cadena was born in Piedrahita, Avila, Spain in 1542. He traveled with his parents to the Viceroyalty of Peru in 1556 and two years later settled in the city of Cuenca in present-day Ecuador. In 1563 he was appointed Treasurer of the Royal Treasury in New Alcaide of Zamora, in southern Ecuador. The following year he appears as a witness to the merits and services of Diego Hernández de Serpa, about whom he wrote the poem. Three years later he joined expeditions against the indigenous rebels of Valladolid, receiving payment in an encomienda. In 1583 he was appointed captain general of the city of Loja. One year after assuming the post of Deputy Corregidor y Justicia Mayor of the city, he serves as a Lieutenant in the defense of the coast against the attack of the English fleet of Commodore Thomas Cavendish. In 1592 he participates in the raising of the *alcabala* (10% sales tax) in Quito. Seven years later he received the appointment of Captain in his defense of Callao. In 1603 he was confirmed as Deputy Corregidor of Loja and Zamora. Three years later he is listed as treasurer of Loja and Justicia Mayor in the same city. He was also author of a treatise on colonial administration sent to the Council of the Indies (Menéndez Pelayo 69). His date of death is unknown (Ojer and Subero 117-27).

Born in 1510 in Palos de Moguer, Spain, Diego Hernández de Serpa travels with his family to America in 1524. Accompanying Diego de Ordaz on the Orinoco expedition in 1531, he lives in Santa Marta four years later and in 1544 he moves to Panama and then travels back to Spain. Two years later he joins the fleet of the Viceroy of Peru Pedro de la Gasca and returned to America as part of the troops fighting the rebellion of Gonzalo Pizarro in Peru. In 1549 he receives permission from the Audiencia of Santo Domingo for the conquest of Guiana, but it is revoked. Later a resident on the island of Margarita where he was appointed mayor and Ordinary War Captain of Maracapana, in 1552 he begins the expedition to El Tocuyo, and is one of the founders of Nueva Segovia de Barquisimeto. After residing in Quito between 1562 and 1564, on September 15 of 1563 he provides information on the services and merits to the mayor of Zamora (AGI, Patronato, 156 Legajo, Rama 4). On February 7 of 1564 the town of Zamora writes a recommendation for its procurador Diego Hernández de Serpa (AGI, Quito, 18, No. 19) and on the 24th of September, 1564, Attorney Diego Hernández de Serpa seeks mercy for the church on behalf of the city of Zamora (AGI, Quito, 18, N. 24). The following year he travels from Madrid to Cartagena, where he presents their merits and services. In 1568 he receives the capitulation to the conquest of New Andalusia (Venezuela), and a year later he departs from Sanlúcar de Barrameda with a fleet to conquer the territories of eastern Venezuela. Arriving in Venezuela in 1569, he founded Cumaná. Organizing the conquest of Guiana and El Dorado, he dies fighting against the indigenous Cumanagotos and Chacopata on May 10, 1570, at the Gorge Hoces (Ojero and Subero, 53-99). As Tejedor points out: "Surprise is certainly the personality of the conqueror, because with his great mobility and activity, from the modest-and productive-working carpenter in Cubagua, reached lofty to be named Captain of the conquest of Guiana and Governor of the Cumaná Province "(77).

*Los actos y hazañas valerosas* ... is preceded by an Epistle in 94 verses dedicated to Don Diego de Zúñiga and Avellaneda, Count of Miranda. The letter tries to capture the goodwill of the recipient and at the same time, appeal to the formula of false humility. Furthermore, the Epistle emphasizes the importance of the subject to be treated, according to a formula derived from the rhetoric of amplification and used to glorify and exalt the subject of the poem. Hence, in highlighting the exploits of the protagonist,—the actions of Captain Diego Hernández de Serpa—Pedro de la Cadena creates a heroic poem. The Epistle's structure combines the style of the letter and the dedication. The solemn tone used by the author is a literary convention of the genre and is also due to the social importance of the recipient, which requires the use of strict protocols for the treatment of social time. It should be noted that the solemnity of the tone is linked to privacy because it can mimic the Epistle through the direct style, and is essentially a conversation between two people, temporarily removing social barriers. In addition to the conversational style, Pedro de la Cadena uses other formulas such as rhetorical modesty and dedication. The invocation to the Muses is replaced by a dedication to the Count of Miranda, which an example of the theme of humility. The dedication follows the bipartite formula: "subject heroic feats of praise" (Lara 407).

After the Epistle appears the introito, in which we only find the proposition of the argument. The same model is still an explicit praise of the exploits of Diego Hernández de Serpa. The text recognized the legacy of the epic genre, especially those that address an immediate present (Ojero and Subero 184), and the poet traces the limits of his song. In the poem there are two plots. First, there is a historic rejection of the bygone era, as the poet decides to commend actions which occurred only recently. Furthermore, the poem imitates literary medieval models and incorporates the introductory ritual. The author adopts the conventions of the epic, and through classical allusions, he implies the assertion of the poetic voice. The verb "to sing" is used because it refers to recent events, and thus the author meets the standard of temporal proximity. Pedro de la Cadena insists that his poem is historical and makes clear that he praise Diego Hernández de Serpa. The opening statement of the song follows the pattern of identifying the war hero and defines the protagonist by his courage, heroism and honor (García Soto 52). It follows Virgil's model, but imitation appears to change for the Christianization of pagan epics (Davis 23-26). The poem directly invokes Fame rather than the Muses, and is complemented by the diminishing of the subject, a form of false modesty.

*Los actos y hazañas...* follows the model of Juan de Mena in the *Laberinto de Fortuna* (1446), which addresses the recall of feats through poetry, namely the idea of poetry being able to rescue historical memory. A similar theme is advocated by Fernán Pérez de Guzmán in *Elogio de los claros varones de España* (1452), in which he laments heroic deeds forgotten due to the lack of poets who immortalize the feats of the past. Following these literary models, Pedro de la Cadena tries to rescue from oblivion the deeds of Diego Hernández de Serpa through poetry, and thus we observe the tropes of historical truth and immortalization. The introitus keeps the standard startup called epic monumental division, which provides a wide variety of topics. Hence the mention of the topic *Urbs antiqua fuit* recalling the conquests of Mexico and Peru and highlighting the magnitude of the actions of the Spanish soldiers. This scenario serves to put the life of the protagonist of the poem in the context of the victories of the Spanish Empire (Ojero and Subero 187). The central idea of the passage is to highlight the magnitude of the military actions on the territories of Spanish America, Africa, Asia and Europe. Pedro de la Cadena's universal theme of the work is the poetic cartography of Spanish empire, a resource that serves as a context for the activities of the protagonist, according to the meaning of the laudatory poem. In this story about Spanish victories over the Aztecs and the Incas, the author places the wording of the poem in the Spanish conquistadors, and silences the natives who appear only in an oblique way. The second part subordinates the idea of divine justice and wisdom in order to emphasize the need to write poetry to preserve events and counter human limitation. At the end of the introitus, the author confesses that the magnitude of the feats of the Spanish soldiers in America, Africa, Asia and Europe prevents the creation of a work that can restrict the poem's events and themes merely to the military adventures of the protagonist.

In the composition, Pedro de la Cadena manages to present the actions of Captain Serpa as true feats worthy of a heroic character, and also paves the praiseworthy tone that pervades the poem. Moreover, the text also serves a pragmatic function: to support the protagonist in his claim for goods and privileges for services rendered to the Crown. The poem exhibits a feature of the colonial epic: the literary elements are removed from reality because the author uses as an immediate source the merits and services of Diego Hernández de Serpa, consulted between 1563 and 1564. This predominance of realism in fiction that distinguishes the American epic poem is an example of the relationship between discursive genres, and historiographical and literary texts dealing with the conquest of America. At the same time it confirms that pragmatism prevails in epic poetry, which does the same service to the chronicles, and in this case supports the claims made by Captain Serpa for services rendered to the Spanish Crown. This function is mediated through the use of flattering language, where hyperbole is a rhetorical element of poetic language: "and I would say are the top / of courtly chivalry, / and worthy to enter the court / immortality as you celebrate "(Ojero and Subero 180). This poem can be seen as a commisioned poetic memorial, since it is a rewriting of the petition Diego Hernandez de Serpa filed with the Court, but introducing some major changes and several additions, among which are the admonitions and moral inclusion of additional details in the story of the protagonist.

*Los actos y hazañas valerosas* ... is the first epic poem dedicated to the territory of New Andalusia (present-day Venezuela) because it precedes *Elegías de varones ilustres de Indias* by Juan de Castellanos (1589) (Restrepo 29-71). Among the features of the text by Pedro de la Cadena is the historical representation of the facts, since they favor the information from the relations of merits and services of the protagonist. That is, the historical model becomes more important when compared to poetry, and this element is a point of convergence with the medieval epic. Moreover, the originality of the author is evident in the repertoire of rhetorical tropes and motifs used in the poem, which incorporates the new American Spanish poetic tradition, particularly the inclusion of words in indigenous languages as Uyapari, Cubagua, Chalcoma, Maracapana, Guyana and Tocuyo to refer to place names in Venezuela. The composition is based on a dual structure, which favors a historical reading of the poem. Also, the model appears Virgilian due to the presence of a hero who achieves social advancement through the pursuit of fame according to the ideal of the Spanish conquistador. The interpretation by the poet represents an idealization of historical facts, which sometimes alters the history in terms of poetic truth. For example, Act VII tells of Hernández de Serpa's participation in the war against the Caribs, something that does not appear in any historical document. The work of Pedro de la Cadena shows the ability to produce epic fiction with an ideological function (Quint 103) to promote the story of a feat to cover other aspects of greater importance than the violence of conquest. Thus the poem can be read as a pretext to describe the conquest as a heroic action. The composition also represents an attempt to create a fictional alternative to the discourse of history because Diego Hernández de Serpa is made a hero, in contrast to the historical documents that never mentions him in a prominent role. In this sense, the poem is also involved in creating the "myth of the exceptional men" (Restall 1-26), thus raising the importance of the protagonist of the poem.

In the tradition of imperial domination, *Los actos y hazañas valerosas* ... follows a linear teleological structure as befits the epic of the victors (Quint 9-10). The story begins with the hero's family in Spain and traveling to Venezuela, and culminates with the battles against the Indians and Africans in Act XVII. The formulas of the discourse of poetry present a poetic truth that seeks to replace the official story, and it is precisely at this moment of tension when the text shows how poetry rewrite the discourse of history. Innovation in the representation of reality is another contribution of epic genre in America, a change which also affects the problem of truth in poetry. This is a historical fact related to the conquest of America as the poetic form used to illustrate and justify conquistadors' dispatches from a literary point of view. In this way, the author attempts to enhance the aesthetic and moral character of Diego Hernández de Serpa in the conquest of Venezuela. In carrying out this task, embellishment plays a key role; it is follows the organization of the poem and the presentation of the subject, which mimics a temporal order similar to the historical events recreated in the poem. This model also contains a historical poetic appeal that derives from the medieval literary tradition, renewed in American poetry.

The poem by Diego de la Cadena not only mimics the historiographical and literary models, but also includes a title that provides a link between legal rhetoric and composition. The title deeds and acts intend to give authority to the poetic text through legal discourse, and thereby legitimize the content of the poem by using a rhetorical strategy that seeks to attract more attention and recognition for the work. The linking of the poem with the legal discourse implies that the author attributes to his work an authenticity that goes beyond the literary formulas because ultimately the text is based on the authority of law and the material strength of the Spanish bureaucracy. Among the new possibilities offered by the legal discourse of epic poetry is the function to support the claims of rights and privileges to those conquerors who felt neglected by the Crown, a function similar to the epic poems on the conquest of Mexico (Mazzotti 147-49; Pullés-Linares 79-102). Written with aesthetic merit to support the claims of its protagonist, Pedro de la Cadena's poem was filed with the Court and resulted in Philip II granting Diego Hernández de Serpa a Capitulation for the conquest of New Andalusia in 1568. In this regard, *Los actos y hazañas* ..., despite being a little known text, highlights the importance and prestige enjoyed by epic poetry in the sixteenth century.

# CHAPTER 4

## Female Agency and Araucanian Ghosts: The Work of Mourning in *La Araucana* (1569) by Alonso de Ercilla

A countrapuntal reading (Said 59) of Alonso de Ercilla's *La Araucana* uncovers aspects not considered in previous readings of this text, particularly the critique of the destructive consequences of war through the depiction of female sorrow. I consider this the most important aspect of the poem since it uses the rhetoric of mourning to question the epic discourse of the victors. At the same time, however, these two cantos serve to highlight another aspect not considered by previous studies. I refer to the existence of a metonymic vacuum in the passage that conceals an important cultural void in the poem. This lack manifests itself as the absence of any reference to Araucan funerary practices that are the very reason for the lament of the poem's indigenous female character. In my view, Ercilla's omission serves as an allegory for an important exclusion that transcends the poetic text. I speak of the exclusion caused by the conquest and which signified the destruction of the Mapuche culture.

Cantos XX and XXI of the second part of *La Araucana* tell the story of Tegualda and Crepino. While the poet-soldier Ercilla is keeping watch in the middle of the night, the young Tegualda appears alone, desperate to find the corpse of Crepino for burial. The Indian maiden finds her deceased beloved on the battlefield and carries the body away to be buried. The scene of relatives seeking mercy to bury their dead has a long literary tradition (Priam, Antigone, Argia), but unlike other textual models, Ercilla portrays mourning differently. Cantos XX and XXI of *La Araucana* are modeled on Book XI of Virgil's *Aeneid*, and on Book XII of Statius's *Thebaid*, in which appear scenes of collective burials of anonymous soldiers. Moreover, the precursor of the unburied body dates back to the epic models of Elphenor (*Odyssey*) and Palinuro (*Aeneid*), because these figures are imaginary projections of the torments and sins of the living. It has been argued that an additional influence is canto XIII of Ariosto's *Orlando Furioso*, which tells the story of the tragic love between Isabella and Zerbino. These models appear to be Ercilla's principle sources of inspiration in cantos XX and XXI of *La Araucana*. Hearkening back to the beginning of canto XI of the *Odyssey* in which a shadowy night foreshadows a descent into the world of the dead, canto XX uses the night as the initial setting for the story of Tegualda. The nocturnal scene echoes conventions of the beginning of the elegy, whose aim was to prepare the minds of readers. Ercilla relates that at the most arduous moment of his watchmen duties, Tegualda appears at dusk, just in "el cuarto de la prima" (Ercilla 568). The poet tries to stay awake by walking from one side to another, and ironically notes that the causes of his sleepiness are due to a soldier's exhaustion and hunger, and not the delicacies of good food. The difficulty of introducing this lyrical scene manifests itself as the poet's reluctance to begin narration since he hesitates when referring to his mental state at the start of the scene, giving the impression that this particular story is only a dream. This hesitation to commence occurs at night, and recalls Garcilaso's second elegy. Ercilla's scene has as an antecedent not only in the model of the soldier at rest, but also in generic indeterminacy, which translates into the doubt and delay that mark the beginning of the canto. In directly introducing the reason for the poetic pause, the passage imitates aspects of Garcilaso's *Eglogue* III. The imitation of the arms versus letters trope, expanded by our poet from Toledo, clarifies the transformation of the oneiric theme in *La Araucana* in a poetic dream episode, namely the instant when the imagination allows for a lyrical scene to be interwoven within the epic. The narrated episode is a poetic fantasy because, according to the writer, "divisar lo cierto no podía" (Ercilla 570); in other words, the history of Tegualda must be told from a framework of uncertainty and mystery in which facts cannot be completely clarified.

The poet sets the start of his canto at night, so that this nocturnal episode charged with silence and stillness is conducive for the evocation of the funeral theme and of Tegualda, whose appearance is preceded by the overpowering vision of physical death that the poet describes in all its crudeness: "vi que estaba el un lado del recuesto/lleno de cuerpos muertos blanqueando,/que nuestros arcabuces aquel día/habían hecho gran riza y batería" (Ercilla 570). Such a vision alludes to the depiction of an enemy's abandoned corpse destroyed by animals, which represents the antifuneral theme in the Preface of the *Iliad* (Redfield 328). The absolute contrast between the darkness of night and the whiteness of the skeletons represents the image around which Ercilla develops his canto. The scene opens with a description of the post-battle landscape in which the sense of sight dominates. From the depiction of the skeletons of dead Araucans, it is possible to trace the trajectory of the poet's emotions and feelings as a journey that moves between darkness and light, between life and death; the poetic voice accepts this cleavage with great intensity in order to tell a distant tale that becomes its own story. In this canto, the young soldier departs from the labors of war to usher in a poetic voice that arises from a deep emotion. In the episode of Tegualda, the canto's climax is marked by Ercilla's meditation in a subdued tone, giving the impression that the author is in a conversation with himself and thus enabling him to adopt the form of poetic soliloquy followed by a dialogue between characters. Ercilla explicitly points to the emergence of the poetic moment that arises immediately in response to the terrifying image of the "cuerpos blanqueando" (570).

From this moment forward begins a devastating portrait painted through the senses of sight and, in particular, sound. In the middle of an absolute darkness noises and sighs are perceivable. In these stanzas, the visual and the auditory coexist at first, but sound gradually assumes a dominant role. In the growing emphasis of sound over sight, Ercilla begins to listen to the story of Tegualda, a character whose essence is defined by her own narrative voice. Since Tegualda is identified for the first time with the phrase, "medrosa voz" (Ercilla 570), the young indigenous woman is identified as only a voice, and since she is a literary figure defined only by her voice, lacking a portrait or physical description, she is painted as an ethereal character, namely as a ghost that emerges from the world of the dead: "donde vi entre los muertos ir oculto/andando a cuatro pies un negro bulto" (Ercilla 570). The scene of the emergence of Tegualda is similar to the moment of the ghost sighting because in both episodes sight prevails despite the fact that what is seen is somewhat indefinite and uncertain.

Ercilla frames the action in an unspecified area in which the boundaries between reality and fantasy are erased: "La noche era tan lóbrega y escura/ que divisar los cierto no podía" (570). It is precisely in this space of uncertainty that the poet sees a vision so horrific that he is compelled to make a desperate attack, which in turn is interrupted by something unusual. This is the scene of encounter with the phantasmagorical figure. The indigenous maiden appears in the midst of the darkness and identifies herself as a woman. The emergence of a female character at night recalls a Petrarchan technique (Manero 548), and allows us to appreciate how Ercilla uses the conventions of Petrarchan poetry to show the contrast between light and shadow. With the image of Tegualda as a "vision" illuminating the darkness, the possibility occurs to narrate a love story. Also, the emergence of the female figure reverses the order of the canto, because prior to her presence in the poem, the description of the natural elements was prevalent. Because the poet reproduces Tegualda's lengthy speech recounting her life, the emergence of a female character marks the moment in the text when humans come to occupy the center of the action. She encounters Ercilla after abandoning her community to enter the enemy camp, forced to identify herself as women. This act of identification allows the poet to contemplate the female figure as a mortal being and abandon the idea of her being an actual ghost.

Tegualda appeals to the common theme of the lady in distress, because her goal is to try stop the armed violence by using mourning discourse to counter the destructive images of male power. However, in this apparently traditional representation of the sexes, the burden of proof is shifted to the main cause of war that Tegualda reveals with the phrase that defines the precise origin of the conflict: "los términos lícitos" (Ercilla 571). This quote points to the central theme of the conquest: the lawfulness of armed actions undertaken by the conquerors against the Araucans. Ercilla implicitly raises this theme in the passage where Tegualda speaks. The idea of the legality of military action in the poem is linked with the theme of justice, as confirmed when the Indian states: "Mira que aquel que niega lo que es justo/lo malo aprueba ya y se hace injusto" (Ercilla 571). The proximity of the two most relevant legal terms used in debates on the conquest (lawfulness and justice/licitud y justicia), also serves to show the moment of crisis in the poetic voice. The moment is focused around a widow and the unburied corpse of her husband, killed during a battle between Spaniards and Araucans that had happened a few hours earlier. The splitting of poetic subjectivity is twofold: first, it is linked to the feminine because the speaker is a woman, and second, it showcases an ethnic difference because Tegualda is indigenous, highlighting an otherness of ethnicity and of gender that offers a different perspective to that of the soldier Ercilla.

The soldier's encounter with the lady has its origins in Petrarchan tradition of the "armed lover" (Manero 78), which is used in the poem as a literary topic coinciding with the poetic world of narrated facts. Ercilla elaborates the episode extensively, because instead of being a love story between a soldier and lady, the poet transforms the encounter into the story of the unfortunate love of Tegualda, which in turn serves as a framework to the bucolic and elegiac nature of the canto. The passage is interspersed with stories of love and death, imitating the pastoral idyll that is doubly idealized, if we take into account that the context of the narrative is framed by the war between Araucans and Spaniards. The passage in which Tegualda tells the story of her relationship with Crepino in an idealized world that can be interpreted as an eclogue, despite ending with a war and the death of her beloved.

The rhetorical strategy of a fracture which gives voice to the enemy, places poetic discourse in extreme doubt, a fact which manifests itself in the unrest of a woman who suffers at the loss of a loved one. The character of Tegualda achieves a psychological depth that surpasses any other female figure that appears in the poem. The main lament begins with the phrase that describes her as "widow, miserable, sad and unhappy" (Ercilla 571). The intensity of the initial speech gives Tegualda a resolve necessary to carry out her mission: the rescue of her beloved's body at any price. Ercilla amends the Virgilian model when he uses the terms "barbaric war" and "tyranny" to refer to any action that seeks to prevent the rescue efforts and when he bestows piety upon the young Araucan, a quality reserved for Aeneas.

It must be kept in mind that Tegualda's claim recalls the themes of love poetry. The request of Tegualda reveals the essential paradox of lament according to classical epic tradition. It also draws attention to the insistence of the poetic voice in using legal jargon to situate the position of Tegualda with respect to the body of Crepino. That complaint reaches its poetic apex with the statement: "Deja buscar su cuerpo a esta alma mía" (Ercilla 571). As Lerner points out, this phrase is modeled after the works of Petrarch and Garcilaso, and suggests that the beloved woman is the soul of her lover. Ercilla inverts, however, the traditional relationship in which the man was the active subject, because in *La Araucana,* the feminine soul undertakes the search for the male corpse (Ercilla 571). Tegualda is presented to us as a ghostly figure that assumes the role of a wandering spirit, searching for the body of her beloved. This is precisely the aspect which caught the attention of several critics. In his study on the work of Ercilla, Menéndez Pelayo hints at the figure of the spectrum or ghost which characterizes the young Araucan, when he refers to the shadows of Glaura, Guacolda and Tegualda (295). It is very likely that Ercilla takes his phantasmic figure from the lyric tradition, one rife with ghostly images of heroic love and abundant in French romances, Provencal poetry, and in the works of Dante and Petrarch.

The poet establishes an association between the complaint and the lawsuit, which serves as a prologue to the lament of Tegualda and prepares the mind of the reader to hear the sad story. The maiden begins her narration using the epic technique which involves interspersing the lament with a story detailing the death of Crepino. This results in the narrative mediating the past life of the deceased with the present moment of death (Derderian 25). A part of the mourning structure for Tegualda, the portrait of Crepino's most relevant moral and physical qualities emerges in the poem. The presence of these characteristics is a means to evoke the dead and an attempt to give substance to the spirit, thereby converting the deceased into a ghost (Derrida 72). The section ends with a funeral scene that indicates the time of departure and separation, namely the farewell of a beloved whose body is brought to burial. This depiction ultimatetly fosters a judgement about life. Tegualda recalls how she met Crepino and the brief moments of happiness they enjoyed before his death; finally she reflects on the ephemeral nature of life facing the mortality of human beings. The use of the word "infelice" will be repeated several times in this canto and the next, which recalls the same epithet used by Virgil to refer to Dido. Tegualda, like Dido, becomes a widow since her marriage with Crepino barely lasts a month: "Hoy hace justo un mes, ¡oh suerte dura,/qué cerca está del bien la desventura!" (Ercilla 584). With these lines Tegualda references the topic of the *mors inmature*, a recurring theme in classical and medieval literature derived from the model of canto VI of the *Aeneid*, particularly the passage that tells of Aeneas's visit to Anchises (Ramajo 316). The above verse also makes use of the stylistic appeal of antithesis to establish the contrast between two moments in time, stressing one of the most relevant aspects of the elegy (Núñez 178).

The statement by Tegualda implies recognition of her fatal condition, and it is when the acceptance of one's own mortality is the basis of the relationship that the individual engages equally with the living as the dead (Harrison 70). Through Tegualda's sorrow, Ercilla introduces to his readers the topic of death using the language of lament, implying that anyone who has the ability to speak on this issue and its consequences, shares with the rest of humanity a theme that unites all people: mortality. The self-referentiality of sorrow is what gives the voice of Tegualda a universal quality. In addition, it must be kept in mind that the funeral rite is open to participation by acquaintances and strangers alike. Through the mourning of Tegualda, Ercilla anticipates and experiences the moment of his own death. The poet imagines the atrocities of war to project the pain of young Araucan maiden, which lets the author develop a sense of community deeper than that derived from the political ideas or social conventions of his time. Such a sentiment is based on the inevitability of death shared by all individuals.

It must be acknowledged, though, that the episode stems from the tradition of prestigious epic scenes, the importance of Tegualda's story is that it constitutes an example of counter-discourse that delivers a devastating critique of war and death while offering a meditation on the ontological status of literature. On the other hand, it draws attention to the coincidence of Tegualda's mourning with the same characteristic that Fantham indicated with respect to Statio's *Thebaid,* a classic epic poem in which the lament serves to question the hero's pursuit of glory and is a rejection of war (226-232). The sorrow of the Araucan introduces the topic of death and what has been lost as a result of warfare; in that sense, it provides a different perspective to the official version of the conquest that corresponds to Ercilla the soldier. Ercilla ends canto XX with the epilogue and the reason for his own tiredness (Goic 17-34), a rhetorical strategy that goes back further to the Greek custom that stated that sorrow had to be suspended until nightfall (Holst 204). The poet includes as an introduction in canto XXI—where he concludes the story of Tegualda—a defense for women, although that mimics the tradition of Renaissance and classical works and also fulfills the more important goal of being a rhetorical embellishment.

The exordium of canto XXI outlines a defense of the woman, consequently changing the viewpoint of the poet. After giving Tegualda, the female character, a voice, Ercilla makes known his own views on women, thus shifting the attention from the male hero Crepino to the indigenous heroine. This change is carried out using a vocabulary derived from the tradition of epic poetry, particularly from Virgil's *Aeneid*. In canto XXI, Ercilla begins to use expressions and phrases that are associated with Aeneas and take on a new connotation in the poem. Particularly striking is the repeated use of the word "pious." The reference to Tegualda's action as "obra tan piadosa," serves to establish a contrast between the words and deeds of the epic hero Aeneas in the episode of Dido. The description of the young Araucan as "infelice bárbara hermosa," is an elaboration of the characteristics of Dido, who Virgil calls "unhappy Fenis" (Virgil 158), but in the version that Ercilla develops, the beauty of Dido extends into the territories of the New World and becomes barbaric. Used in antiquity to refer to people who were not Roman, barbaric is used in the American context to designate the Indians. Canto XXI is a rewrite of the poem by Virgil, and accordingly provides an alternative version to the theme of Dido. Ercilla begins this section of the poem with a process culminating in the dedication of an entire song to the figure of Dido. By giving the character of Tegualda greater relevance in the narration, the role of canto XXI serves as a preamble to this episode. In the first 20 songs of *La Araucana,* the young indigenous female character is the most developed in the work. In the introducion of canto XXI, Ercilla presents his sources of poetic imitation, which establish the contrast between the various worlds of the characters created by Virgil. The criticism of the classical poet develops from the opposition that occurs between the words and actions of characters.

For Ercilla, the love of Tegualda is strongest because it transcends death, as the remembrance of those moments spent next to Crepino and in search for his body is testimony to the depths of her feelings: "¿Quién de amor hizo prueba tan bastante?" (Ercilla 587). That is why the poet appeals to the topic of fame, which connects to the false humility as part of a defined writing project— developing a character of literary significance. Ercilla alludes to the theme of poetry as immortalization by following the models of Homer, Lucan and Juan de

Mena (Lida 285). Furthermore, in his annotation to this canto, Lerner makes reference to Garcilaso's *Eglogue I* as being a possible influence of this episode in *La Araucana* (Ercilla 587). Regarding the previous literary tradition, this passage of Ercilla demonstrates a fundamental difference as a result of imitation of Ariosto, especially of canto XXXVII of *Orlando furioso* (Lida 86). Ercilla was inspired by Ariosto's canto, but further develops his ideas to mention an array of famous women of antiquity, which in the case of the Italian poet boils down to the mention of a few isolated names and a complaint about the lack poems praising women. Instead, Ercilla is more eloquent in his defense of women, an essential aspect that distinguishes him from Ariosto. The listing of heroines plays a different role in the work of Ercilla, as it appears to serve as an introduction to Tegualda's sorrow, and in this sense her position within the poem acquires greater significance.

In the literary tradition of lament, the ennumerating of male heroes was a rhetorical device which developed into the topic of *memento mori*, a key component within the genre. The rhetorical strategy consisted of referring to celebrities with the aim of establishing a comparison with the dead (García 72), characterized by the listing of deceased heroes and learned men in order to elevate the character of those to which the lament was dedicated. In this regard, one can recall the famous register of the ancient emperors that Jorge Manrique includes in his poem. According to this tradition and the theme of the canto (the death of Crepino), it is expected that the enumeration be composed of the names of illustrious men since the deceased is male. Ercilla transforms this topic and transfers praise from the male character of Crepino to the female figure of Tegualda. One might ask why the author amends the meaning of *memento mori* in *La Araucana*. This topic requires some transition verses to prepare the minds of the audience and thus capture the attention of readers. Precisely, the role that the catalogue of heroines plays within the poem is to introduce the character of Tegualda from a more important perspective, following the literary tradition. There is however a model in epic tradition that Ercilla could have imitated besides those mentioned by Lerner and Lida; I refer to canto XI of the *Odyssey*, which contains a list of fourteen heroines.

Upon presenting Tegualda along with other illustrious female literary figures Ercilla's aim is to highlight the exceptionalness of Tegualda. The purpose of the author seems to elevate Tegualda to the same category as other heroines of the most celebrated literary tradition. Ercilla includes Dido on the list of famous women, thus anticipating his own disagreement with Virgil in the phrase: "la fenisa Dido/ a quien Virgilio injustamente infama" (588). Beginning with a public critique and ending with acts of rewriting, this critique demonstrates a divergence which will manifest itself as a rejection and surpassing of the Virgilian model. However, the new interpretation of the story of Dido—possibly meant in this passage as an extension of the history of Tegualda— has a more complex impact in Ercilla's work as a whole. The author uses the same technique to tell the story in two cantos (XXXII and XXXIII) in the third part of *La Araucana*. In these cantos dedicated to Dido, Ercilla develops his work with great artistic beauty accompanied by a complex structure that occurs at the end of the canto XXXIII. Embedded within canto XXXIII, there appears the story of the capture and death of Caupolicán as a preamble to the tragic canto XXXIV. Ercilla rewrites and corrects the pioneering work of Virgil, introducing the story of Dido as an apotheosis for those who sacrifice themselves for love. In this regard, it would be desirable to formulate the following questions: Why does the capture of Caupolicán appear in the same song? How can we interpret the death of Caupolicán after reading the story of the sacrifice of Dido? In the poem, women's stories are closely related to the figure of the ghost, because they always feature death as a central aspect of the story. The figure of the ghost also has another possible meaning in the poem if interpreted as an allegory of what is hidden, and of the exceptional and extraordinary. The episodes that deal with female characters in *La Araucana* introduce the notion of the ghost within a theoretical framework, in particular the explanation offered by Rabaté that the ghostly figure is produced less by the loss of an object than by an awareness that the character was always destined to die because of his uniqueness (xxii).

The presence of female figures in the work of Ercilla constitutes a unique aspect in the epic tradition, thereby requiring a careful study of the role that sorrow and poetry from a feminine perspective takes. Needed is a careful analysis of the lament of women and their link with the transformation of biological death into human death, a process similar to engendering life after death, which translates into a metaphor for the soul with its images, memories and voices. The novelty here is that unlike earlier models, this is a story about ghosts, namely about the search for the dead and memories of the deceased. Tegualda's journey through the world of the living is represented by her encounter with the poet-soldier Ercilla. Her wandering, story and dialogue with Ercilla are located within this dimension of reality; at the same time, though, the young Araucan inhabits the world of the dead through her memories of Crepino. It is this story of life with her beloved that gives the character of Tegualda greater psychological depth as a female figure who speaks from pain, tells anecdotes of another previous life—one prior to death and war. It is when Tegualda speaks most of her deceased husband that we can best view her as a female character. Moreover, the initial description offered by Ercilla of the young maiden is the typical depiction of a ghost scene that highlights wailing, shadows, white dresses and dark night. Through the voice and the gaze of Ercilla, Tegualda arrives from a nocturnal space which is also the realm of death. From death, the ghostly figure of Tegualda enters, and to death she returns carrying the corpse of loved at the end of canto XXI. Narrated over two cantos in the poem, the wanderings of the young native have only one aim, to recover the body of Crepino. To achieve her goal, Tegualda has to convince the soldier Ercilla to allow her to search for her beloved's body among the unburied corpses. The story of the lovers concludes with the discovery of the body and the scene of lament of the young Araucan. This scene introduces a change; since Tegualda has had no success finding Crepino's body on her own, she enlists the aid of a few sharecroppers and eventually Ercilla declares that he himself will participate in the search. The intervention of the poet-soldier is an element of great importance because it transforms the depiction of sorrow and ritual of enemy burial. According to classical epic tradition, a marked distinction between the victors and the vanquished was most important since those who had been defeated also lost the right to perform the ritual of burying their dead. In addition, the passage in which Ercilla accompanies Tegualda mimics the episode of the *Iliad* in which Achilles consoles Priam over the death of Hector.

In the scene that recounts the discovery of the corpse of Crepino, the poet's gaze focuses on the shattered body of the young Araucan: "...el sangriento cuerpo helado,/de una redonda bala atravezado" (Ercilla 590). Although the author makes no comment when he finds the corpse, the visual power of the scene is clear and reinforces the image of death and mutilation of the body as an additional difficulty affecting the mourners, in particular, Tegualda. Crepino's maimed body is linked on the one hand, with the theme of disfigurement of the body in the classical epic, and on the other hand with Ercilla's personal experiences in the war against Araucanians. In canto XX, violence intensifies, culminating with the image of the shattered body of Crepino. That scene is a sublimation of the topic of the difigured corpse that appears in Homer's work, because the corporeal mutilation is related to the attempt to eliminate the possibility that the hero will be remembered and thus endure in the memories of future generations (Vernant 332). Precisely, the lament of Tegualda exists to preserve the memory of her loved one for posterity, and hence the funeral rite fulfills the role of attempting to preserve the name of Crepino. It must be kept in mind that the classical epic, the ritual of burial and the poem dedicated to narrate the feats of the hero, played the role of conserving the hero's memory (Vernant 333). Therefore, this allows us to understand the insistence on Tegualda to recover the corpse of Crepino, carry him to her people and give him the honor he deserves. The rescue of Crepino's body also aims to avoid the disfigurement of the body and its destruction. In the classical epic, the mutilation and desecration of the defeated enemy's corpse not only meant that the defeated became some unknown mass, but also meant that the enemy was denied a "beautiful death," an act that ultimately sought to erase collective memories of the deeds of the enemy hero (Vernant 336). These are the literary topics that Ercilla manipulates and come to him through the literary tradition of classical and Renaissance epic poetry. The passage of the desecrated body of Crepino also has a close link with the experiences of Ercilla as a soldier. In this regard, Murrin notes the objections that Ercilla made in regards of the excesses of war and analyzes the third part of *La Araucana* as an study in visual horror" (210). Beginning from Crepino's death scene, one can observe a deliberate and premonitory image of horror which speaks to Ercilla's disapproval. The total destruction of the body of the young Araucan through armed violence represents the first moment of criticism of the excessive use of firearms, and here Ercilla uses the techniques of drama and interrupted speeches to give expression to the intense emotions and altered state of the poetic voice. The poet interrupts more than once the narration of the scene while also transferring the poetic voice to

Tegualda through the technique of distancing. The rhetorical strategy of distancing reveals Ercilla's intention of detaching himself from the role he played in the battle which resuted in Crepino's death.

The scene of Crepino's disfigured corpse is the rhetorical strategy that Ercilla adopts to show the disastrous consequences of violence, and thus make the audience visualize the shattered bodies of the fallen and wounded in combat. The poet relies heavily on the description of the defeated enemy corpse, but due to the magnitude of destruction and havoc caused, cannot include detailed descriptions of the wounded. For Ercilla, portraying this scene of desolation is more important than any moralizing speech (Murrin 215). It is also a part of the theme of lament to capture the readers' attention through details, and thus affect their emotional state. Hence, the issue of disfigurement of the body provides "a test of visual horror of the situation" (Race 93).

The verses of canto XXI correspond to the so-called ending formulas of elegiac poetry, whose main objective was to capture the maximum sympathy from readers through the use of an exaggerated pathos (García 117) combining the pain and anger ("horrendous fury") over the loss of a loved one. The stanza of Tegualda's mourning which depicts her weeping— "flujo de vivas lágrimas bañaba"—aims to intensify the pathos of the scene, since it is more effective to hear waling from relatives after illustrating Crepino's maimed body. Ercilla removes himself from the scene and by way of poetic fiction cedes word to Tegualda. The withdrawal of the poet is expressed as a moving away from the focus point, presenting the scene as a portrait of the actions caused by pain and despair of Tegualda. From this point the episode takes on the plastic quality due to the strong visual impact. The image of the face of Crepino as "marchita faz desfigurada" is related to the funerary theme of the withered flower as symbol of a premature and unexpected death (Ramajo 319). However, it has greater significance for the poem's symbolism that follows the mourning tradition dating to the classical epic. Ercilla echoes this symbolism in the passage where symbols of intense pain range from the desire to die to the previous stanza's expression of the attempt to commit suicide, since we are told, "furiosa por morir," because it is Tegualda who inflicts injuries on her own body: " echaba/ la rigurosa mano al blanco cuello." Such an image is derived from the theme of insanity caused by an excessive pain (García 155), which in most cases is manifested as a change in emotion. The issue of self-harm that appears in the line, "no perdonaba/al afligido rostro ni al cabello," correponds to the topics of "mesarse los cabellos" and of "rasgarse la cara" (García 157), and have their origins in the classical epic tradition where mourners cut their hair during the funeral (Redfield 324). Finally, the passage concludes by reiterating the immense desire to die, a rhetorical strategy that accentuates the inconsolable grief of the young Araucan.

At this point we must now move from a textual reading to a cultural reading of the poem. This reading entails taking into account the broader cultural context of the work's production and including other cultural traditions, in this case the Mapuche culture because it is the culture represented through the characters of

Tegualda and Crepino. A cultural reading of the text allows for other views and other interpretations. In my opinion, the story of Tegualda and Crepino does not end with the farewell of Tegualda. The poem presents only a part of the story that is an allegory because of its exclusion; there is another story not told, corresponding to a culture denied or silenced. What is beyond the text of Ercilla? To answer this question it is first necessary to ask: How important is the body of Crepino in the poem? Why does Tegualda insist on rescuing the body of Crepino? The answer to these questions leads us then to another scene outside the text.

I refer to the Mapuche funeral which, though never explicitly mentioned, appears to be allegorized through the body of Crepino. Now let's see what Ercilla missed about Mapuche culture in his poem. To understand the other part of reality that Ercilla never knew, we must focus our sights on Tegualda and follow her with our imagination beyond the pages of the poem. Ercilla was not familiar with this other reality consisting of the daily life and cultural practices of Mapuche society, though it did exist. Tegualda needed the corpse of Crepino because funeral rites have a symbolic function of separating the living from the dead, that is, they serve to separate the image of the deceased's body from the world at the time of his death. We must separate the deceased from his remains so that after death his image has its place in life, that is, in our memory (Harrison 148). Tegualda needs to carry Crepino's remains to the village of the Mapuche where relatives will conduct a funeral ceremony known as a *kurikawin*, or wake of the dead (Faron 94). Needed for the start of the ceremony, the corpse is placed next to the *Chemamull*, an anthropomorphic sculpture in wood (Aldunate 91) that functions to preserve the memory of the deceased. Once the *Chemamull* is in place, the next stage of the ceremony takes place. Called *weupin*, it consists of speeches by relatives and friends who make eulogies to the dead and recall his greatest achievements in life (Faron 97). Finally, the *Chemamull* is placed next to the tomb to mark the place where the body is buried. It is important to remember that the ceremony is inconceivable without the body. During the *kurikawin*, the presence of a human body is essential in order that later there be a symbolic transfer to the *Chemamull*. The absence of the body implies a crisis for the Mapuche family because it prevents the consummation of magical-religious practices established to guarantee the future welfare of the community. In traditional Araucanian culture, these rites were necessary because death was conceived as a powerful balancing element between the forces that control the universe. A funeral rite, therefore, ensured that the spirit of the deceased, after a period of wandering among the living in the form of an *am*, undertook a journey to the *wenumapu*, or other world, joining the ancestral spirits mourned by those living (Faron 68). However, if the bereaved neglected these rites, the *am* could be captured by any *kalku*, a group of witches dedicated to turning a spirit of the dead into an evil spirit called a *wekufu* (Aldunate 90-92), considered responsible for calamities and bad deeds among the Mapuches. The *wekufu* assumes different manifestations according to Mapuche beliefs, including the form of a wicked ghost called a *witranalwe* that persecutes people at night (Faron 71, Dowling 21). For this reason Tegualda needed to recover the remains of her husband; she needed to ensure that the savior *kurikawin* would allow Crepino's spirit to rest in peace and form part of the *pillán,* the pantheon of Araucanian warriors (Aldunate 86).

In conclusion, we can say that through the character of Tegualda, Ercilla develops a complex reflection on the relationship of lament and its critical role in the devastating consequences of war. Tegualda's mourning is also a meditation on the ontological status of literature and its relationship with death. In this sense, the theoretical figure of the ghost is used to explore the role and functions of female sorrow in the work of Ercilla.

# CHAPTER 5

## Phantom Authorship, Amerindian Bodies, and Slavery in *Nuevo mundo y conquista* (1580) by Francisco de Terrazas

The epic poem *Nuevo Mundo y conquista* by Francisco de Terrazas appears inserted within the *Sumaria Relación de las cosas de la Nueva España con noticia individual de los descendientes legítimos de los conquistadores y primeros pobladores españoles*, written by Baltasar Dorantes de Carranza around 1604 and published in 1902. The original manuscript of Terrazas's poem is lost and there exist only 23 fragments included in the manuscript of Dorantes (Lasarte 45-66). Terrazas begins his poem with a rhetorical declaration expressing the impossibility of recording all the feats of Hernán Cortés to explain the technique of beginning in *medias res*. He apologizes in advance for the silences that appear in the poem about aspects of Cortés's life mentioned by other chronicles and histories of the conquest of Mexico. The first stanza of the poem ends with a mention of the literary theme of poetry's incapability of depicting Cortés's victory. The allusion of Terrazas in the first stanza of his poem to the classical epic *("arma, virumque cano,"* Virgil) reflects a rejection of the protasis of the past of the epic genre, seen as a distant mythology when compared to the historical reality of an immediate present (Prieto 53-54). Also in the expression of Terrazas, there is a rejection of Ariosto (under Ercilla's influence: "No las damas, amor, no gentilezas"), which highlights the affirmation of the poetic voice that is born of an immediate present. It is a restrictive or negative poetics defined by something else, not by itself. The poet sets limits for his canto and says what he will not record in order to differentiate himself from other poets and distinguish his work. While Ercilla in Canto I of *La Araucana*, consciously opposes Ariosto's famous lines and says that his poem is about war and not love, Terrazas affirms that his desire is to depict only the actions of Hernán Cortés. It should be noted that this aim of Terrazas has two levels. On a historical level is the longing of the past moments of military campaigns during the conquest of Mexico. On a poetic level is the struggle against epic models and the search for his poetic voice. It is this need to impose the present onto the poetic voice which restricts the canto with a promise that, like in Ercilla's work, will also be unfulfilled because the poem mentions other topics besides Cortés.

The proemio of *Nuevo Mundo y conquista*, like other epic poems, adopts the trope known as monumental demarcation. Terrazas sets limits to his canto, but in practice deals with other aspects beyond the central theme. The proposal incorporates metaphorical structure within the introductory ritual, not the rhetorical structure exemplified in words such as singing, love, weapons... that recall Virgil ("*armas, virumque cano*"), Ariosto ("*Le donnes, cavalier, l'arme, gli amori,/ Le cortesie, l'audaci impresi io canto*") and Ercilla ("No las damas, amor, no gentilezas"), among the best-known models. The canto's imitation of Virgilian arms is changed from a vision that subordinates the classical pagan techniques to the transformation proposed by Tasso called the Christianization of the epic (Caravaggi 199). The octave shows imitations of Ercilla, particularly the negative first part that repeats the Ercillan verses. The initial statement follows the Virgilian model of individualization of the war hero in the figure Hernán Cortés. The negative statement by Terrazas, though, is only part of the imitation of the introductory ritual. Terrazas begins listing what he will not write about, particularly "miraculous events", or mysterious, supernatural events that go beyond the historical facts.

The theme of *La Araucana* is the conquest of Chile without an individual hero, while in *Nuevo Mundo y conquista* the main hero is Hernán Cortés. Despite some formal resemblance between the prologue of *La Araucana* and of *Nuevo Mundo y conquista*, there is a fundamental difference between the two poems that is represented by an individual hero defined by his name and attributes: "magnanimous", "courageous". The image of Hernán Cortés developed by Terrazas will serve as a model for other poets, including the title of another epic on the conquest of Mexico. The initial declaration of the canto in *Nuevo Mundo y conquista* is modeled after *La Araucana*, which in turn is a replica of the subject matter of *Orlando Furioso*. The first verse refers to the topic of surrender to the new and the need for new themes, typical of epic poetry that echoes the model of Camões: "Cessem do sabio griego y del troyano" (71). The prologue of Terrazas is part of epic poetry tradition, though the assimilation of readings and models show varying degrees of influence ranging from familiarity with certain works, to an echoing of, allusion to and misrepresentation of poetic models produced by limited readings. The author's reference to "canto" has its genealogy in the *Aeneid*. Virgil uses the first person singular which represents the invention of the subjective epic (Nuttal 22). It is through the repeated assertion of the poetic voice in first person, of a rootedness in the Virgilian tradition, and of clear echoes of Camões that Terrazas defines his poem. This implicit invocation of previous authors is complemented by the topic of false modesty and devotion (Curtius 129 and 586). Terrazas insists that the argument of his poem is historic and true: the conquest of New Spain. Like Ercilla, Terrazas highlights the collectivity represented by Spanish soldiers. This aspect serves the pragmatic aim of reclaiming the rights of the descendants of the conquerors of Mexico (Mazzotti, *Agencias* 148). The first stanza of Terrazas is opposed to the statements of Ercilla because it is an embellished canto of multiple themes. Similar to Virgil, the verb *cantar* is in the present eventhough it refers to past events, serving to connect with the theme of reclaiming by descendants of the conquerors. Thus Terrazas includes the topic of the present facing the past in the second stanza, following the epic technique of introducing a hidden proposition in code. The second verse of the Prologue alludes to the notion of *Urbs antiqua fuit* (Nuttal 25) to depict the ancient cities of Aztec civilization. Terrazas speaks of the magnitude of Cortés's actions and demonstrates that the profound structure of the poem corresponds to the magnitude of the conquest that led to the conquering of millions of indigenous foes.

*Nuevo Mundo y conquista* remains the topic of ekphrasis similar to *La Araucana* I, 6, and the *Aeneid* I, 12-20. This description is very panoramic since it barely mentions the geography of the territory of Mexico. Terrazas imitates Ercilla's prothasis starting the first part of the octave in a negative way and the second part in a positive way. The prologue emulates Ercilla only in the declaration, since it does not correspond with development of the poem as a whole. Faced with the unsung heroes of Ercilla, Terrazas counters the individual hero of the poem: Hernán Cortés. The poem also deals with other themes because it includes references to the expeditions of Francisco Hernández de Córdoba and Juan de Grijalva, which were prior to the mission of Hernán Cortés. There are also fragments dedicated to Diego Velázquez, Francisco Morla, Jerónimo de Aguilar, the sinking of ships by the conquistadors on Cortés's orders, the love episode between the natives Huitzel and Quetzal, among other topics. The second stanza passes in quick succession over the conquered Mexican territory. Terrazas highlights the magnitude of the feat of the conquistadors to universalize the theme of the poem. Thus Terrazas responds to Ercilla by pointing out that the conquest of New Spain is more important that the conquest of Chile and also frames the encomiastic meaning of the poem as well as its pragmatic role of supporting the claim for goods and privileges by the descendants of the conquerors. Terrazas puts the wording of his poem in the Spaniards and unlike Ercilla, makes no mention of Indians in this section of the poem, because the natives appear sublime in comparison to the victorious actions of the Spaniards over the enemy. Trace the contrast between the ambiguous statement in *La Araucana*,—"que a la cerviz de Arauco no domado/ pusieron duro yugo por la espada" (Ercilla 77)— corresponding to Ercilla's historic moment and the total defeat and final conquest of Mexico that is expressed in political ("rendidos reyes"), military ("ejércitos vencidos a millones"), and religious ("dioses postrados falso del profundo/ a quien sacrificaban corazones") terms. The verse ends with the theme of human limitation because the author insists on writing, which helps poetic recall of the facts, but is subordinate to the idea of justice and divine wisdom (Caravaggi 185). That is why the topic of weapons is not an earthly issue like in the work of Virgil, Ariosto, Camões or Ercilla, but an expression of a divine willingness that is insinuated in the idea "of the divine mind", a symbol that later appears expanded inthe poem. The poetic prologue of *Nuevo Mundo y conquista* does not follow the introduction format of Virgil's classical model of the proposition, namely the invocation to the Muses and dedication to Maecenas (Prieto 16). In the poem of Terrazas, we only find the proposition of the argument, but no invocation to the muses as part of the process of the Christianization of the epic according to the precepts of Tasso. The proposal follows the negative model of Camões and Ercilla, (Prieto 51; Goic 310), which serves as a renewal of old themes and the search for novelty in the field. In his argument Terrazas announces that he will talk about the exploits of Cortés and his soldiers. The main argument of the first octave summarizes that the agenda of the poem falls between the models of the epic tradition and the novelty to record something completely new. In this way the poem accomplishes the goal of introducing new subjects, with the aim of capturing the reader's attention. The dedication assumes the rhetorical figure of prosopopeia because it is aimed at Cortés, who died during the time when Terrazas wrote the poem. The invocation to the Muses (Curtius 329) is replaced by a dedication to Cortés in the thematic tradition of humility (Lara Garrido 180; Curtius 669-71). Terrazas, unlike Ercilla, says that it is impossible to praise the feats in all of their glory because they are ultimately miracles that only God can understand. The poet assumes a restrictive poetics in compliance with the precept by Juan de Mena and Ercilla which express the need to recall famous events for the goal of articulating communal ideals. Terrazas thus presents a poetics of the community expressed through the complaints of the conquerors and their descendants.

The dedication follows a bipartite formula (Lara Garrido 407). This invocation is more elaborate because next to the topic of *mediocrita mea / Maiestas tua* (Curtius 129-30), Terrazas introduces the main goal of poetry as being one of immortalization (Curtius 669-71). Terrazas understands that the very magnitude of the conquest hinders the creation of a work that could represent this event poetically. The stanza fifth is an apostrophe to Cortés and replaces the praise of Muses. The third fragment includes the expedition of Francisco Hernández de Córdoba who discovered the Yucatan in 1517. The mention of this expedition perhaps has the same purpose of the first letter of account of Villarica, which is to serve to counteract the position of Velázquez. Although the poem describes the facts after the time of conquest, its point of view favors the descendants of the conquerors of Mexico. There is a coincidence in these verses between the names of the conquerors mentioned by Terrazas and those whom Dorantes mentions in his chronicle. This is one of the passages in Terrazas's poem that has a direct intertextual relation with the chronicle of Dorantes. Among the Spaniards who participated in the expedition of Hernández de Córdoba, the poem of Terrazas and the chronicle of Dorantes mention tbe following: Gaspar de Ávila Quiñones, Benedicto Cuenca, Alonso de Ojeda, Diego de Porras, Alonso Ortiz de Zúñiga, Martín Vázquez and Miguel Zaragoza:

> After the happy ending of the war
> to Cuba was to chosen people;
> in a short time saw the whole land
> surely serve peaceful,
> But as the foundation that is err
> go wrong does the following,
> for gold mines found
> slaves to be started.
> The cause is not for me to judge

even this is the place to be decided
if the time could justify
and the other is just prevented;
well know that after examining
was rigorously prohibited
although the remedy in time be sent
repair the islands were not enough (Terrazas 28).

The passage mentions directly the problem of slavery. Terrazas is one of the authors who stated that the initial purpose of the expedition of Hernández de Córdoba was to search for slaves to work in the gold mines in Cuba. Other chroniclers such as Angheria, Oviedo and Bernal Díaz do not mention the issue of slavery, though Las Casas denounces slavery as the general reason for the mission: "Que les diese licencia para ir a saltear indios dondequiera que los hallasen" (II, 163). For his part, Gómara explains the reasons which inspired the expedition of Hernández de Córdoba: to bring slaves from the Guanajos islands (85). In this section of the poem Terrazas seems to follow the thesis of Gómara, because he mentions the same ideas:

Before decayed in such a way
in short this happy state,
that of the Indians with havoc and death
an infinite number was finished,
and as no one turns from gold to
the rustic benefit of livestock,
to work the mines was the trace
to hunt certain people (Terrazas 29).

Gómara also provides more details about the indigenous people of the Guanajos islands, stressing the peaceful nature of the natives: "Están los guanajos cerca de Honduras, y son hombres mansos, simples y pescadores, que ni usan armas ni tienen guerras" (85). Terrazas alludes to the legality of the expedition, since Velázquez had no authority to organize expeditions that questioned the rights of Diego Columbus. This point forms part of the allegations employed by Cortés against Velázquez. Terrazas refers to the three organizers of the expedition: Francisco Hernández de Córdoba, Cristóbal de Morante and Lope Ochoa of Caicedo. The hidalgo Cristóbal de Morante, a native of Medina del Campo and inhabitant of Sancti Spiritus in Cuba, was then captain of one of the ships of Pánfilo de Narváez. Morante drowns when his boat sinks in a storm on its way to San Juan de Ulúa in April of 1522 (Thomas 360). Lope de Ochoa died in May 1522. Francisco Hernández de Córdoba, born in Córdoba and a resident of Sancti Spiritus in Cuba, died in May 1518 as a result of wounds sustained during the expedition. Terrazas reproduces the number of members of the expedition—"110 soldiers "(29)—and mentions other prominent figures of the expedition like the pilot Antón de Alaminos and the supplier Bernardo de Calzada. The latter may have been a rhymed modification of Bernardino Iñiguez de la Calzada. Native of Palos and participant in the expeditions of Christopher Columbus, Antón de Alaminos was the pilot of the expedition. He traveled with Pedro Camacho, a native of Triana in Seville, and Juan Alvarez, the "manquillo" native of Huelva (Díaz del Castillo 4). Angheria refers only to the three leaders of the expedition and the 110 soldiers (397). Also offering the same names, Gómara includes the pilot Antón de Alaminos and offers a fact that other columnists do not mention: "Alaminos brings a boat with bread, and tools to work in the mines" (86). Bernal Diaz, possibly obligated by the mention of Gómara, also spoke of the Velázquez's vessel, which was handed over to the expeditioners on condition that they used it to "cargar los navíos de indios de aquellas islas, para pagar con indios el barco, para servirse de ellos por esclavos"(4). According to Bernal Díaz, however, soldiers rejected this idea of going to enslave Indians.

The main source of Terrazas's poem is Gómara's *Historia*, because of all the chronicles and stories of the conquest of Mexico this work serves as a main source for the historical actions in the poem. In certain passages, the historiographical model of Gómara is transformed through techniques of imitation of the epic. In this case the changes serve to offer a different interpretation to the facts narrated by the chronicler. This difference in viewpoint between the chronicle and Terrazas's poem is another example of the emergence of a sense of community amonge the Creole descendants of the conquerors of Mexico, a group to which Francisco Terrazas and Baltasar Dorantes Carranza belonged. *Nuevo Mundo y conquista* is an example of the relationship between historiographical and literary genres in texts about the conquest of the Americas. An important feature of the colonial epic poetry is the inclusion of aspects of historical reality with elements of literary tradition. The predominance of realism over fiction in epic poems is a trait from classical models, particularly of the *Pharsalia* by Lucan (Avalle-Arce 19-20). The writing of the epic genre in the Americas reaches new levels of sophistication, as can be seen in the passage from the poem where Terrazas makes criticism of slavery a moral admonition, and where the poet used the rhetorical question as a technique to disguise his viewpoint on a compromising issue during the colonial era.

# CHAPTER 6

## Aztec Ghosts and the Voice of Death in Romances and Songs Related to the Conquest of Mexico

Most *Histories of Latin American literature* agree that the first romance sung on American soil appears in Bernal Díaz del Castillo's *Historia verdadera de la conquista de la Nueva España*. But they overlooked that this romance is also the first-known evidence of satiric poetry in the New World. Bernal recalled in Chapter XXXVI of his work that during the journey to Mexico on April 21, 1519, a group of sailors and soldiers, veterans of the expeditions of Hernández de Córdoba in 1517 and Juan de Grijalva in 1518, show the details of the Mexican coast to Cortés. The remarks of the sailors and soldiers cause the intervention of Alonso Hernández Puertocarrero, who recounts in a casual tone the Montesinos romance of chivalry to Hernán Cortés. Puertocarrero begins his speech with a comment that serves as a framework for the poem. Before starting the analysis of Bernal's passage, it is necessary to mention some features of satiric poetry. One of the two essential elements in this genus is the subject of enunciation, and Arellano states the importance in this poetry of condition of enunciation and the social role of the character. It is important to know who is the character and what is its role in this context. In that sense, it is necessary to describe briefly Hernandez Alonso Puertocarrero and understand why he uses a satirical tone with Cortés.

In *Conquest. Montezuma, Cortes and the Fall of Old Mexico*, Hugh Thomas gives some information about Alonso Hernández Puertocarrero and his relationship with Hernán Cortés. Originating from Medellin, he was cousin of the Earl of this city and nephew of the judge Céspedes, and therefore was a prominente person. Cuba was in a place with 150 Indians. Although Puertocarrero had no military experience, Cortés sought his involvement in a Cuban matter, and even paid part of his expenses. This explains the degree of intimacy between Cortés and Puertocarrero since the beginning of the expedition. Thomas also recalled that Puertocarrero, together with Francisco de Montejo, was one of two attorneys sent by Cortés to court to seek the royal benefit for his company (146).

The first letter sent by the expedition from Mexico regarding the Town of Veracruz on July 20, 1519, details the objectives of these two representatives of the Town before the Court. The letter of the Cabildo de Veracruz speaks not only to prevent the appointment of Velázquez as governor of the new conquered territories, but goes further and calls for his dismissal on account of all the charges that relate to Cuba. The tone of the letter is accusatory and asks for a lawsuit against Velazquez. The Court received the letter from the town of

Veracruz with a rich sample of gifts sent by Cortés, who, after waiting two months, sought an opinion from the Court to set a precedent in the conquest of America. It is undeniable that the decision of the Court was a matter of consideration. The main purpose of the letter was to support the position of Cortés. As Thomas points out in *The Spanish Empire,* it was not the moment for a real definitive answer, and the ambiguity of the Court's decision allowed Cortés to consolidate his position compared to that of Velázquez (600).

Returning to the moment of poetic exchange between Cortés and Puertocarrero in 1519, it should be remembered that this year coincides with a period of great importance in the spreading of the romancero between 1511 and 1550. This process of revival began in 1511 with the publication of the *Cancionero General* by Hernando del Castillo, and further transmission of romances comes from those printed in the collections of documents, and of course from the oral tradition, maintained by the memory of generations. The immediate outlook for the conquest of Mexico shows that at the time, it was fashionable to paraphrase each romancero verse in a gloss, i.e. contrahacerlos. No matter the subject it was necessary to clarify the various parts of the romance, and as a demanding literary game, as the work was a display of ingenuity for the audience. Popular ballads, and in particular their altered versions, emphasized the author's wit and put to test the memory of listeners.

The romance that Puertocarrero recites is a short snippet of the first four verses of the romance of Montesinos, belonging to the so-called Carolingian chilvalrous romances. Here a brief passage of the romance of Montesinos to better understand the satirical intent of Puertocarrero:

> Behold France, Montesinos
> Behold Paris the city!
> Behold the Waters of the Douro
> Which flow down to the sea (Thomas 173).

According to Bernal Diaz's version, Puertocarrero only needed to recite the first four verses of the romance for all easily to recall the poem. There was no need to say more because the lines set the mood for the listeners who remembered the following stanzas where he spoke in detail of the wealth of the city and the main enemy. Puertocarrero in a satirical manner says: "I say that you are looking at rich lands and may you know how to govern them well" (Thomas 173). Cortés easily understood the reference to the material wealth that the romance imaginatively re-created, but transposed the events to a real and visible present right in front of the eyes of the conquerors on the Mexican coast. Alongside the satirical innuendo, there is an allusion to the governor of Cuba, Diego Velázquez. The effect creates a satirical image of a hateful Velázquez, making him a dangerous foe capable of being "defamed by its language" to snatch the spoils of conquest. As noted by Victor Frankl: "It is demonstrable that the great idea of Cortés, the disruption of Velázquez's instructions, appealing directly to the King as the guarantor against any rule of particular interest, is known and understood within a group of *cortesianos* through a set of literary allusions" (32).

Puertocarrero's comments prevents Cortés of the danger and clearly calls for action against Velázquez. The famous "know how" not only involves the art of politics, but in particular is aimed at Cortés promoting the expedition before the Spanish Court. This seems to be the final scope of the satire: the attention of Cortés on the need to care about the results of military conquest, and to have the savvy necessary to protect the economic rewards of the expedition. Through satire Puertocarrero informs that it is necessary for Cortés to wage two battles at once. The first is the military conquest of Mexico, and the second is the defeat of intrigue and legal maneuvering by Velázquez. Letters of Cortés's to the king and the embassies of the two attorneys with gifts for the court tell of Cortés's attempts to secure the final victory against Velázquez. The verse that Puertocarrero makes satirical, not only brings the spirit of chivalry by creating an atmosphere of complicity with the mocking that everyone could identify, but it also serves to identify publicly though indirectly that Diego Velázquez is an enemy of Cortés and of the entire crew. The latter is what Cortes understands and takes most of the form with a brilliant response. Cortés said: "Let God give us that good fortune in fighting which he gave to the paladin Roland. After all, with you, and these other gentlemen, as leaders, I will easily learn how to manage things" (Thomas 174). Cortés replied with a verse that is a direct allusion to the romance of Gaiferos when a saddened Countess tells her son how his father was killed.

Cortés uses the *romancero* to denote complicity and also sends a key message against possible divisions and betrayals of the nobles still loyal to Velázquez. Cortés understands the satirical hint of Puertocarrero, but first answered wisely that he needs military victories that appeals to the divine favor, and thereafter (in mocking tone) will take care of the rest. Again, as in the case of Puertocarrero, he here seeks to include everyone in the fight against Velázquez, and especially appeals to the gentlemen of the expedition. He closes the sentence with a double sense of fun: "I know well." In this idea of understanding or agreement between the acute response to Puertocarrero and the final exchange of romances, which creates a subversive atmosphere against Velázquez and end with the support of most of the crew (Frankl 32). The Spaniards were so familiar with the *romancero* that they not only remembered and quoted the verses from memory, but also remade and parodied them in new and different historical contexts. The weight of literary tradition is so overwhelming, that everyone understands the double meaning of Puertocarrero's words. The satire takes a literary re-elaboration as a mockery of the knightly romance of Montesinos, in which Alonso Hernández Puertocarrero transforms the romance to suit the new situation. In this case, the text is a parody of the romance of Montesinos in the satiric words of Puertocarrero.The tone changes the meaning of the text because it transfers the space-time romance of Montesinos from Europe to America. In this way, the allusion to the city of Paris refers to the idea of an artificial wealth established around the past, to tradition, and to order established by law and custom to which we must obey and respect.

Although the original romance mentions the code of chivalrous conduct, the American version subverts this code, or more precisely, modernizes chivalry so that the notion of nobility is determined by individual performance and not merely by one's origins or social background. The romance with satirical intent seems to open a new path of social advancement absent in the peninsular romance. In the satiric text the word "land rich" refers to natural beauty, the area of nature where European culture is absent and consequently the European legal order. In this space before the conquest the rules and regulations of the European society no longer function. The Mexican lands appear as the space of the future, and alludes to an opportunity where "know how" allows Cortés to directly question and take the initiative, thus proclaiming himself political leader of the new Mexican territories. Parody suggests that Cortés immediately breaks the vassal ties with Diego Velázquez, governor of Cuba. When Puertocarrero remakes the romance and turns Velázquez into his "mortal enemy" in allusion to the a character in the poem, Cortés understands the parodic sense that Puertocarrero creates because his answer is direct and to the point: "God give us luck in arms as the paladin Roland, who in the rest, taking your worship and other gentlemen by gentlemen, know me well understand."

Governance will be the main political task and its implementation occurs from the letter he wrote from Veracruz. I think this poem is interspersed with burlesque poetry because poetry is a kind of inspirational political maverick with subversive implications. The subversive feature of the poetic exchange between Cortés and Puertocarrero undermines the value system of the time and represents a breakdown of the colonial legal order. This anti-system aspect is hidden under the mechanism of the satirical-burlesque joke against Velázquez by using conventions of the romance. The personal tone of the romance functions as a rhetorical approach to the listeners, thus facilitating the formation of an artificial and temporary sense of collective involvement that creates the need for Cortés to respond with two verses and an addendum which Puertocarrero questions and answers.

The first letter sent by the expedition from Mexico regarding the Town of Veracruz on July 20, 1519, details the objectives of these two representatives of the Town before the Court. The letter of the Cabildo de Veracruz speaks not only to prevent the appointment of Velázquez as governor of the new conquered territories, but goes further and calls for his dismissal on account of all the charges that relate to Cuba. The tone of the letter is accusatory and asks for a lawsuit against Velazquez. The Court received the letter from the town of Veracruz with a rich sample of gifts sent by Cortés, who, after waiting two months, sought an opinion from the Court to set a precedent in the conquest of America. It is undeniable that the decision of the Court was a matter of consideration. The main purpose of the letter was to support the position of Cortés. As Thomas points out in *The Spanish Empire,* it was not the moment for a real definitive answer, and the ambiguity of the Court's decision allowed

Cortés to consolidate his position compared to that of Velázquez (600). It is not a simple act of anticipation of Cortés, as Frankl (32) says, but a detailed knowledge of how Velázquez acts, and in particular, how Cortés tackles the complex political and personal relations of the governor of Cuba. Puertocarrero parodies Cortés's sharp critical response, giving the romance an undeniably dangerous political situation hidden within a playful exterior. The situation is dangerous because it alludes to Cortés's actions which could be considered treasonable against Governor Velázquez. Therefore, the exchange of romances between Cortés and Puertocarrero also acquires a subversive nuance because "when it celebrates burlesque values opposed to the official ideology dimensions becomes potentially subversive" (Arellano and Roncero 13). The cutting action is subversive because he said the romancero's key intention is to break the vassalage with Velázquez; this action is not only an act of treason, but a subversive act because it opens the way for future actions of disobedience of vassals to their lords. Cortés's subsequent actions against Velázquez show an understanding of the legal significance of the relations between lord and vassal. That is manifested in the development of a subtle justification of an act of rebellion against the governor of Cuba. García Gallo explained the legal reasons for Cortés's decision to break his the subordination to Velázquez in a direct vassalage to the King (42). But legally, there was also a provision in the contract of the Cortés, which could be used to justify the break with Velázquez. This provision can also be understood as a hint of romance in the words of Montesinos, "that if the King took a salary / everything can be revenge," and it refers to the effect that Velázquez was also a royal subject and his interests and privileges were subject to royal interests. That is, the royal interests were more important than the relationship of allegiance between Cortés and Velázquez, and for that reason, Cortés could break any treaty or contract with Velázquez. The letter from the cabildo of Veracruz provides important details to understand the strategy of Cortés to become independent from the authority of Velázquez. The conversation began with a comment in jest and had a serious subversive background because Cortés announced plans on the way to break his allegiance with the governor Velázquez. The atmosphere of complicity and humor are produced due to the conspiracy and the support of the members of the expedition.

# CHAPTER 7

## Spectral Texts and Ghost Author in *Historia de la Invención de las Indias* (1525) by Fernán Pérez de Oliva

There have been a host of texts published about the Columbian expeditions, but *Historia de la Invención de las Indias* by Fernán Pérez de Oliva have not received the same critical attention. This is evident in the study of the Columbus expeditions, which is the key to understanding the process of the conquest of America and the Spanish Renaissance. It should be noted that the textual production related to Columbus has had significant attention from historians such as Manuel Ballesteros, Juan Manzano, Antonio Rumeu de Armas, Juan Pérez de Tudela, Demetrio Ramos, Juan Gil and Consuelo Varela, but the relationship between the work of Fernán Pérez de Oliva (h. 1494-1531) and Pietro Martire d'Angheria (1457-1526) has not been studied with the same attention in recent years.

In 1965 José Juan Arrom published the first edition of *Historia de la Invención de las Indias*. Arrom's introduction explains the evolution of the text and tells the most significant events of the historiography on Pérez de Oliva, starting with the work of Atkinson, Henríquez Ureña and Maeso. Because of its importance, the work of Pérez de Oliva should have engendered several critical editions, but except for the Arrom editions of 1965 and 1991, and the Ruiz Pérez edition of 1993, the amount of critical studies has been bleak. Thus, among the most pressing problems are the need for new editions from reliable manuscript to correct the errors of previous editions, and the call for clarifying reading errors. A uniform standard edition is warranted to fix the problem of multiple interpretations or misreadings. Arrom consider only Pérez de Oliva's narrative of Columbus; while Ruiz Pérez includes the text of Cortés and the conquest of Mexico in addition to the Columbian text. In my opinion, it is necessary to recover the integrity of Pérez de Oliva's two American texts and overcome the fragmentation of manuscripts created by the people who auctioned them. It is important to clarify that the unified edition of Pérez de Oliva's two manuscripts relating to America also has important implications in the interpretation of the work because it will demonstrate a greater intellectual significance of his work.

Greater attention to the literary historiography and the historical context will help to present a text with fewer errors in interpretation. Because there are few readings, the lack of comparative analysis between the base text and critical commentary on the dearth of alternatives matches and leads to the lack of a systematic and uniform treatment of the text, especially the modernization of spelling. It is necessary to establish a uniform standard of editing and avoid errors of interpretation. Another related aspect is due to the lack of studies on

Spanish Humanists, with the exceptions of Rico, Yndurain, Cerrón and Ruiz Pérez, among few others. The existing Pérez de Oliva's editions suffers two types of errors. The so-called linguistic and factual errors. The main consequences of poor fixation of the text is bad annotation and interpretation. But in the case of American texts is also essential the rigorous historical data.

I will analyze the three major editions of *Historia de la Invención de las Indias* to see the development of the theory and practice of editing Pérez de Oliva's work. The first edition of Oliva's text was published by José Juan Arrom in Bogota in 1965. Arrom's paleographic edition is an annotated transcript and coincides with the work of other American chroniclers. Arrom only accepted the type of editing known as the paleographic transcripts, which involves the maintenance of almost all graphs with only three exceptions: all abbreviations are resolved, some are bound separate words, and capitalization and accentuation are modernized. Although Arrom maintains an absolute fidelity to the text, he yields to a particular reading. A major problem posed by this editorial approach is the inability to accurately reproduce all types of antique printing. That is, an issue of this kind can lead to confusion because of the diversity of text types used in printing and the modern reader's lack of familiarity with these conventions. Another aspect that makes this practice very difficult is the case of each text that demands different types of letters, as opposed to a uniformity of approach still widespread in modern editions today.

Arrom's edition is preceded by an introductory study and a codicological description analyzing the binding, paper, watermarks, fonts, and the foliation of the manuscript. Another important theme of Arrom's introduction is the authorship of the work. This section discusses the history of the manuscript and its interpretation about the authorship of Pérez de Oliva. Arrom clarifies that the current manuscript is a copy prepared on the basis of a lost original. Arrom starts a textual annotation consisting of 197 non-consecutive notes, some of which cause confusion in certain passages. The notes combine philological, historical, anthropological and cultural annotations, although some philological notes are incorrect, as pointed out by Rico in a review of this book in 1967. In my opinion, the greatest deficiency in the annotation is in its linguistic and literary explanations relegated to second place against the historical and anthropological details. The historical notes match Pérez de Oliva's text with passages from the works of Angheria, Las Casas, Oviedo, Gómara and Hernando Colón.

In 1991, Arrom published a second edition of the *Historia de la Invención de las Indias* introducing major changes. First, it modernizes the paleographic text and transformed it into a modern edition. According to Arrom, the 1965 edition "establish[ing] the authenticity of the manuscript" had been fulfilled. Another change is the modernization of the spelling, the removal of the annotations to the transcript and outside references originally made by the copyist. Arrom explains that he keeps records and updates the historical notes to the passage of the ethnographic narrative of Fray Ramón Pané devoted to the indigenous cultures of the Caribbean. The most significant changes are 169 consecutive notes.

Striking that despite the years and the vast amount of new research, Arrom does not change the preliminary study of 1965, only briefly appending it. The result is a reader-friendly edition that still retains the original tone of the first edition. Arrom's proposal to insert this work into the canon of historians and chroniclers of the conquest of America has not had great reception among Latin American colonialists in the U.S. academy. The main consequence of this neglect is a lack of studies and projects devoted to the work of Fernán Pérez de Oliva. This silence and oblivion is critical because the most important works on this author come from researchers in Spanish universities, in particular from Golden Age specialists who explain the appearance of the edition of Ruiz Pérez, causing an extensive critical activity around Pérez de Oliva that adds to the list of important contributions from Francisco Rico, María Luisa Cerrón, Consolación Baranda, and José María Vega, as well as from José Luis Fuertes, and Joseph Pérez in philosophy and history.

In 1993 Pedro Ruiz Pérez published the third edition of *Historia de la Invención de las Indias*. This edition started in 1987 with the publication of the book *Fernán Pérez de Oliva, and the Crisis of the Renaissance,* and a lengthy series of articles devoted to the life and work of Pérez de Oliva. The 1993 edition is preceded by a lengthy study entitled "Between History and Literature" that summarizes the critical model Ruiz Pérez uses. The study is divided into two parts. The first analyzes the biography and the author's work within the historical context of Renaissance Spanish literature, and the second part examines in detail the relationship between literary and historiographical discourses of the Renaissance and its impact on the work of Pérez de Oliva. Ruiz Pérez first proposes a new edition unifying the two texts, and he then proposes a modernization in spelling. He seeks to clarify the abbreviations, contractions and errata, but does not intervene in the textual gaps. Ruiz Pérez's edition has 143 notes. He clarifies that he has dispensed with historical, geographical and ethnographic annotations because they appear in the edition of Arrom. The contribution of this new edition is a collation "of authors who have served as a source direct or indirect to Pérez de Oliva or are very close to his creation" and supplements Arrom's more focused historical sources. The main contribution of Ruiz Pérez is the publishing of the two texts of Pérez de Oliva, capturing well the integrity of the Columbian and Cortés stories that appear as part of a broader intellectual project. It should be noted that the unification of the two texts are based on Pérez de Oliva interrupted writing due to his death. The idea of an unfinished manuscript and the providential encounter between Hernando Colón and Fernán Pérez de Oliva are the main topics of critical discourse around the work of the humanist. We must move from endless debates about the historical context of the visit and talk to the authors' examination of the text, similar to models of reading in studies of Abellán, Baranda, Cerrón, Ferreras, Rico, and Ruiz Pérez. These readings recognize the cultural production of literary works, including the material reality of the manuscript. The questions and riddles that the text presented to the investigators can only be resolved with the reading of the work and a collation of texts. First, it is necessary to read

*Historia de la Invención de las Indias* with the *Decades of the New World* by Angheria for the same reason that the second reading of the letter from Hernán Cortés is inseparable from the understanding of the history of the conquest of New Spain.

As there is no tradition of the printed *Historia de la Invención de las Indias*, we must read the precursor Angheria to understand why Pérez de Oliva's text is interrupted, creating the feeling of an unfinished story for the modern reader. A brief overview of the editions of Angheria's work shows that since the first translation to "Venetian dialect" was published in Venice in 1504, there exist only nine of the ten books that make up the original work. Also the edition printed in Seville in 1511, which saw the light "against its author" contains only *Decade* I. The edition published in Alcalá de Henares in 1516 have the *Decades* II and III, with the first print approved by the author. The first French translation appeared in Paris in 1532 as an extracted, as indicated by the title.

The work of translation made by Perez de Oliva was not unusual at the time. Since 1530, the *Decades* of Angheria began to be published in full, and the tradition of publishing the first two translations into vernacular languages, the Venice edition of 1504 and the Paris edition of 1532 were also incomplete editions. Now we understand that completion of the manuscript of the ninth narrative in the *Historia de la Invención de las Indias* does not necessarily indicate an interrupted work, but a practice of writing similar to that of other translations of the works of Angheria. In this case, Pérez de Oliva is also consistent with the practice of his time. It is precisely around 1530 that Angheria's work is more widespread because in that year the first edition of his letters is published in Alcala de Henares, as well as the first Latin edition of the eight *Decades*. In 1532 there appears a version in Latin, which was the basis of the first German translation of 1534, preceded by two years by the Paris edition. In the period of writing the *Historia de la Invención de las Indias* between 1525 and 1528, the work of Angheria was not forgotten, but part of an important editorial movement. Moreover, if we place the translation of Pérez de Oliva within the European context, of the Italian translation of 1504, the French one of 1534, and the German one of 1532, the intellectual project of Pérez de Oliva is consistent with problems related to Humanism in Europe beyond the common place of "play on demand" as requested by Hernando Colón. It is not enough, however, to say that *Historia de la Invención de las Indias* is a translation of the *Decade* I. It is necessary to stress that it is an interpretation, and therefore a re-reading and re-writing, of the work of Angheria. Let us not forget that most of the translations in the Renaissance are interpretations. Considering the limits and then variations of the re-writing, it is insufficient to say that Pérez de Oliva's text is an extract from Angheria, and we cannot reduce the analysis to the comparison of certain isolated passages of Angheria. What is at issue, then, is a collation of readings from both texts to see where Pérez de Oliva alters the work of Angheria; at the same time we must pay attention to what is new in Pérez Oliva's text which has no reference in the work of Angheria.

In Book I of the *Decade* I, Angheria explains the route of Columbus since his departure from Spain and his passage through the Canary Islands. The author then suspends the narration on a trip to collate Columbian historiographic narrative of the conquest of the Canaries. Pérez de Oliva did not mention the passage of the Canary Islands by Columbus, neither the story of the conquest of the Canary Islands; instead he spoke of the history of the Portuguese company that puts the Columbian version of the story. The problems of annotation and interpretation of this passage are multiple. The first question is why not mention the Canary Islands and why detail the story of the Azores? Secondly, what is the basic text used by Pérez de Oliva to include the story of the Azores? Thirdly, what does this passage say about the legend of the anonymous pilot? Fourthly, what does this interpolation was the work of Pérez de Oliva or Hernando Colón. That is, maybe it was this reference that Columbus presents near the Portuguese that led to Hernando Colón's decision not to publish this text at a time of Columbus litigation. As Juan Gil says there is no single source in the *Decade* I, but the compilation of various written and oral sources by Angheria made him able to organize a coherent story of the first Columbus expedition. This multiplicity of sources is another common feature in the text of Pérez de Oliva, hampering the interpretation of passages such as the Azores. Until now, there is no mention in the criticism of this passage on the Azores islands that seems to follow the line of argument on the pre-Columbian discovery and the story that appear in the works of Gonzalo Fernández de Oviedo, Hernando Colón, Francisco López de Gómara and Las Casas. To understand the context of the passage from the Azores in Pérez de Oliva, it is necessary to recall Chapter IX of the *Historia del Almirante* by Hernando Colón, known as the third reason and evidence that somehow led to the Admiral's Discovery of the Indies' and mentioning some of the previous expeditions to that of Columbus in 1492.

The practice of travels prior to Columbus shows several examples of Portuguese expeditions to the Atlantic Ocean. The expedition of Diego de Teivo organized by the Infante Don Enrique in 1542, seems to have reached beyond the usual Western for navigation of the Portuguese era. According to testimony in subsequent Columbian lawsuits, it is known that Colón told the pilot of this expedition, Pedro de Velasco, the details. Another important expedition which is organized at this time is that of Fernando Telles, but it does not take place. In 1475, in conflict with Castile, King of Portugal granted a concession to occupy the islands to the west of the Atlantic Ocean to Fernando Telles, but was abandoned because he dies in Setubal's battle in 1477. Another expedition is organized by Portuguese Fernam do Arco Dominguez, who received the 30 June 1484 the captaincy of an island west of the Atlantic Ocean. In 1486 King John II of Portugal granted a royal charter to Fernam Dulmo for the discovery of the islands of the seven cities.

The theory of pre-discovery attains its most complete development in the work of Juan Manzano Manzano, *Colón y su secreto. El predescubrimiento*. The starting point of Manzano's thesis is the Capitulaciones of Santa Fe between Columbus and the Catholic Monarchs. Although Manzano aims to build upon the historical discourse, he in fact employs philological resources, which allow to use rhetorical procedures to create a chapter that serves as proof to his theory of pre-discovery. Manzano offers a tour of the most important exhibitions on the pre-discovery, but never mentions Pérez de Oliva's *Historia de la Invención de las Indias*. Recently, Juan Gil found a document which has similarities with the passage of Pérez de Oliva. This document is a note written by a licensed Tudela in the sixteenth century on the sidelines of Angheria's edition of Seville from 1511. The reading of this note shows that, at the time of Pérez de Oliva's writing, the circulation of different stories about pre-Columbian trips was common, and in particular, the relationship of Columbus with the Portuguese and their possible sources of information. As we do not have a single reliable source for these stories, it is very difficult to establish the authenticity of them. In any future research on Pérez de Oliva's narrative, we should inquire about literary's sources and medieval legends, and to the extent that the archival materials permit, we must uses interdisciplinary readings to exorcise the ghosts in the text, or the specters between history and legend.

## CHAPTER 8

## Literature, Memory, and Mourning: The Trauma of Conquest in *La Florida* (1605) by Inca Garcilaso de la Vega

I read these pages on the Native American leader Vitachuco as a story concerning the sense of defeat, the feeling of pain, and loss, since it can be considered a work of bereavement. In the present chapter, I will not focus on the historiography of the text, or on the historical context (Hudson), or the questioning of the rules of discourse as discussed by an earlier critique (Mora 19-81). I will instead devote my work to reflect on the relationship that exists between language and death in *La Florida*, through a close reading of chapters 20 to 29 that appear on the second book of the work by Garcilaso. This section of the text is marked by violence and the physical destruction of both, its Spanish and indigenous participants. After a reading of the book, one arrives at the conclusion that the main theme in *La Florida* is death, which in turn is related to loss, mourning and memory.

In the chapters analyzed here, Garcilaso narrates the story of Chieftain Vitachuco and of his rebellion against the Spanish conquistadors. In this section, I will discuss who is this Native American warrior Vitachuco, and the relevance of these chapters within the context of the text written by the Inca. According to the reading that I propose, these chapters do not only tells the story of Vitachuco, but also they address more complex issues, such as how to create a narrative about the New World. First, the placement of the chapters throughout the book is based on the objective for achieving a sense of balance and symmetry, demanded by the rules of Renaissance prose. We can begin to understand this issue better, if we established a comparison between the chapters dealing with the death of Vitachuco, and those chapters devoted to the death of the Spanish conquistador Hernando de Soto. The death of Vitachuco is described on chapter 28 at the end of the first section of the work, and seems to be a rhetorical device in order to maintain the structural symmetry of the books, which are divided into two parts. In contrast with the placement of Hernando de Soto's death in Chapter VII in the middle of fifth book (Galloway 38).

Moreover, chapters 20-29 reveal other elusive aspects of the text, as well as exposing the process of the drafting and the drafting the work itself. The Inca begins the narrative by declaring: "The more carefully than he had been writing things that they like and have passed," and in Chapter 27 pertaining to Book II the following statement appears: "Where an objection is answered or opposed." Both instances constitute the most articulate defense of the idea concerning the representation of truth in the work. Garcilaso's ideas on History are part of a rich literary tradition, and contribute to explain rhetorical elements of his discourse. In my opinion the insertion of the author's self-defense in Chapter 27 is unique since it appears intertwined in the story of the Indian Vitachuco. The ideas presented by the Inca in these pages constitute an expansion of the argument in favor of the veracity of the events narrated in the text as exposed previously in the "Preface" and their presence in this section of the book is unusual. The question remains: Why does the author decided to introduce the defense of the truth of the work in this passage? As part of the favorable representation of the native people within the text, Garcilaso's main point in this passage is to demonstrate the rational nature of the Amerindians, which was an important issue of the theological and legal debates held during the sixteenth century. The rhetorical strategy employed by the Inca is based on the direct reference to authorities such as the Father José de Acosta, who wrote his *Natural and Moral History of the New World* to defend his thesis about the humanity of the Amerindians. However, the salient point of the argument is built around the figure of the witness. The literary-legal institution of the witness brings an important change in historiography: the shift of authority in the discourse of history to the testimony given by the witness. As Foucault states the primacy of the narrative based on the testimony of the witness was one of the methods of introducing change in the search for truth, especially in the evolution of process of inquiry, which since 1492 had as the main stage the territories of the New World (48). Hence, throughout his narrative the Inca always relies on an old soldier that participated in Hernando de Soto's expedition (Garcilaso 220). The main ideas of the passage are centered around the witness's perspective, the accuracy of the discourse that presents historical facts and, especially, the emphasis on the distinction established between author and transcriber (*"escriviente"*). The writing of *La Florida* is depicted as a series of tales narrated by the author, whose principal task is merely to transcribe the events dictated to him by others. The textual link that brings together the episodes narrated is writing itself that serves as a way of legitimizing the truth of the story been told. The apology of the book constitutes one of the most renowned topics of the prologues of the period, appearing in several prefaces as well as in different sections of the work. The insertion of the author's defense within the second book serves as a rhetorical device in order to sustain the thesis of the veracity of the story. Therefore the second question introduced in Chapter 27 is the ethnic identity of the Amerindians, from which Garcilaso goes on to prove the thesis of the natives as rational human beings. One more the topic of the limitations of writing appears, but this time it is examined in conjunction with the identity of the subject, and with the expectations associated with the existential position of the individual. In his book, Garcilaso provides the reader with a detailed explanation regarding this matter.

The topic of humility is built around the question of ethnicity and the statement that they both function as ways for supporting the truth of the work while also securing the approval of the reader. As a rhetorical strategy, Garcilaso makes uses of the chiasm to reverse the sequence of ideas in order to take control of the argument. The author provides us with an account of his childhood years in Peru as part of the story he describes the impediments that precluded him from receiving a sophisticated education as the direct cause of the alleged expressive limitations of his narrative. The problem of limits of language to describe the reality of the American territories constitutes a recurrent topic of New World historiography since Columbus. However, in this case the lack of words represents a greater challenge from the perspective of ethnic difference, and the social status of otherness. Such complexity around the issue of the ethnic identity and the otherness of the natives is precisely what establishes the core of the discourse in Chapter 27. Furthermore, the ethnic origin "because I am Indian," not only functions as justification for the implied failure of the precise use of words, but also as a expected response to the queries concerning the position of the "*escriviente*," and how these questions appear in the text that seek to provide the reader with an image of the inhabitants of the New World. Garcilaso is aware of the necessity to present a second argument that validates his position: the dialogue that takes place between the Author and the *escriviente*. This scene introduces elements in the text pertaining to the literary tradition of the dialogue and the preface, which functions as the rhetorical figure employed by the *Hijosdalgo*, and the clerk in *Don Quijote*. Now we can understand the importance of Chapter 27, and why it appears interspersed with the story of the Indian rebel Vitachuco. The main purpose of the chapter is to provide a philological commentary on the problems faced by Garcilaso in his search for new ways of representing the Amerindians. Why do some of the chapters devoted to the fight of Amerindians require more explanations? What is the purpose of insisting on the veracity of these passages? A careful reading of these chapters can answer these questions. It can be concluded that within the overall plan *La Florida*, and the story of the capture and death of its leader Vitachuco, represents one of the best passages within the whole book. These chapters are distinguished by the combination of warfare episodes with the statements made by the Indians, who in this way made available to the reader their thoughts on achieving victory, while also contributing toward a broader perspective on the historical events been narrated, that do not appear mentioned on the pages of other chronicler.

The old soldier in Garcilaso's narrative did not made a direct allusion to the specific episode of Vitachuco, therefore the aim of the author is not to use this event as a rhetorical strategy, that is, to embellish the discourse as it was the case with the interpolated stories. As Galloway points out, most of the war scenes in the text imitate or exceed the norms of Renaissance in Europe. Garcilaso's favorite vehicle for accentuating the drama of the battle scenes is through the portrait of the noble Indian in contrast to his subordinates, usually depicting the natives in a situation of conflict. Often these same Indians are developed into individuals characters in other stories, such as the brave Vitachuco whose plans to attack the Spaniards are revealed to the readers by a series of translators. However, one of these native characters appears in the stories (39).

In my opinion, the events surrounding the figure of the Indian rebel Vitachuco, and the uprising that he led result in a more complex story. By comparing the different *Relaciones* about the expedition of Hernando de Soto, we only found a single word that appears in every edition to designate a town or a territory. For instance, in the chronicle by the gentleman of Elvas, the following reference appears: "a town called Vitachuco" (Clayton 71); in Biedma's text the word is also use to name a geographical place: "Ivitachuco" (Clayton 227); and it the section written by Ranjel inserted into the *Historia natural y moral de las Indias* by Gonzalo Fernández de Oviedo, this phrase refers to a body of water:"the river or swamp Ivitachuco" (Clayton 267). On the other hand, in Garcilaso's chronicle the word Vitachuco conveys two distinctive meanings: First, it is used to name the Indian rebel that led the uprising against the Spaniards; and second, to refer to the village where the battle took place between the soldiers of Hernando de Soto's expedition and the Indians Timucuan. The chronicle do not seem to coincide regarding the name assigned to the town where the battle occurred, since the place is refer to as Napetuca or Napetaca (Elvas), or as Napituca (Ranjel). Furthermore, there is no agreement between the texts concerning the name of the other Indian chief who fought against the Spanish expedition at the battle of Aguacaleyquen.

A comparative study of the chronicles by Elvas, Biedma, and Ranjel allow us to unveil the developing of the story of Vitachuco in *La Florida*. The events narrated began with the departure of the village of Caliquen on September 10, three days after the natives appeared playing flutes, as a signal that they had come in peace to talk with the Spaniards in order to ask Hernando de Soto for the immediate release of their chief, petition that he refused on September 15 at the village of Napetuca. According with the chronicle, there were between 14 or 15 natives who asked Hernández de Soto for the liberation of their leader, to which he replied that the Indian chief will remain until the Spaniards will arrive to Uzachil. Informed by one of his soldiers, Juan Ortiz, that one of the natives have told him that the Indians were preparing an attack against the Spaniards in order to liberate their chief. The same day Soto prepared his troops in secret to defend themselves against the planned attack. Around 400 Indians came carrying their bows and arrows, and two messengers were sent to Soto demanding the release of their chieftain. The governor accompanied by six soldiers arrived with the chief to whom he was engaged in a conversation in order deceive the Indians until he reached the site where he gave the order to attack the natives. Unexpectedly, the horsemen and soldiers hiding inside the village houses ambushed the Indians. More than 40 natives were killed during the attack, while the survivor fled to the lakes where they were able to resist until the dawn of the next day. Eventually, they surrender to the Spanish soldiers with the exception of 12 of the most renowned Indians who died in battle. The governor accompanied by six of his soldiers arrived with the chief to whom he was engaged in a conversation in order to deceive the Indians until he reached the site where he gave the order to attack the natives.

The captive Indians arrange with one of their translator, who was also a brave man, that as soon as the governor come to talk with him, he should hang him with his own hands. When the Indian translator saw the governor he gave him a hard blow in the nose that left the Spaniard laying on the floor surrounded with his own blood. Suddenly, the natives who were imprisoned began an uprising against the Spanish soldiers. Finally, around 200 Indians were defeated and later executed with arrows by the Indians Paracoxi, who were allied of the Spaniards (Clayton 66-69). The *Relation* of Elvas tells the story of the failed attack by the Indians, but according to the text the assault was organized by 14 or 16 Indians.

In a famous passage from Chapter 20, Garcilaso narrates the story of 'curaca' Vitachuco who was angry at the surrender of his fellows Indians to the Spanish soldiers. The Indian leader revealed his anger with an harangue. The words of Vitacucho followed closely several topics derived from the Renaissance epic. First, his speech is related to the first attribute of the epic imagination: its potential for expansion to new regions of the imagination. Such idea appears also in the diary of Columbus's first voyage in 1492, which recalls the famous words of Bernal: "see things never heard, seen and not even dreamed." But perhaps the literary model that the Inca was more acquainted with was the prologue to the *Lazarillo de Tormes*: "I have things so good for identified, and perchance never heard or viewed (Rico 3), which was the most popular at the time. In addition, the principles formulated by the theory of rhetoric also provides examples of this topic, as mentioned in the *Philosophia Antigua Poetica* written by Pinciano. This topic is modeled after the *Laberinto de fortuna*, by Juan de Mena and is the most significant idea that the Inca is trying to convey to the readers. The task to evoking the ancient heroic deeds by means of historiography, that is, writing in order to preserve the historical memory.

The passage from Garcilaso can be placed within this context of literary history, since it alludes to the risk of vanishing into oblivion. By adopting the narrative mode the author explain the circumstances of composition of the work, the topic of preserving the memory of the past deeds through the act of writing, the inclusion of historical truth, and even the topic of immortalization. This motive is also present in the major epic poems about the conquest of America, such as *La Araucana* by Ercilla and *Elegías de varones ilustres de Indias* by Juan de Castellanos.

Garcilaso is aware of the use of the literary topic of memory, which he utilizes in conjunction with the perspective of the eyewitness and both contribute to lay the foundations of his work. Thus, the messengers act as witnesses to Vitachuco's speech, which reaches the Inca through the testimony of Silvestre and the other Spanish soldiers that participated in the expedition of Florida. From a subjective point of view the role played by the eyewitness will be used by Garcilaso to confer authority to his text, while enhancing his credibility with the reader. Such strategy brought described by Rodríguez-Vechini as an author's attempt toward verisimilitude (619). The literary-legal institution of the witness utilized by Garcilaso reflects a major change in the discipline of history: the shift of authority from the discourse of historiography to the testimony of the historical events provide by the eyewitness. As Foucault declares the primacy of the story based on the testimony of the eyewitnesses was one of the most influential instruments of change in the search for the truth, especially during the evolution of the process of inquiry, which since 1492 had as the main stage the New World (48). The witness in this case is also related to the establishment of what is truthful and especially with the position of an eyewitness similar to the one played in the epic genre by Alonso de Ercilla in *La Araucana* when the author claims his poem represents history and is not a work of fiction (Dowling 112 ).

The figure of the eyewitness has a special significance in the life and work of the Inca. I am referring to a series of circumstances that have profound implications for his life, and that since they appeared this time accompanied him until his death. Such outcome is brought about by the a rhetoric of the temporal simultaneity of vision. Therefore, the case of writing about the conquest of Florida and the subsequent defeat of the Native Americans also brings Garcilaso to undertake the venture of beginning to think in a systematic way about the conquest of Peru. The project of writing about other Indians is translated into a process of self-knowledge in which Garcilaso began to accept the fact that he was a direct descendant of the natives of Peru. Thus, the trauma of the conquest that was repressed and transferred in a subliminal way in *Diálogos de amor*, reappears here assuming an exteriority that unveils what was previously concealed.  The memories of the past history of Peru are now merged with the present time of the scene of writing. The comparison established between the with indigenous societies and the trauma of the conquest, represented that which he did not want to think or write about before, but now appears as part of the inquiry itself, and the recognition of his own alterity. This process of self-discovery will culminate in the writing of the *Royal Commentaries*. In Garcilaso's work, memory proclaims through the act of literature, the uses of the word, and the Quechua voices that are incorporated into the text. In certain circumstances, the author's voice refuses to use the words spoken by others; for instance, *curaca* a voice of the Andes slowly prevails in the text when alluding to the indigenous leaders of Florida. The memory of what has been lost brings about feeling of the deprivation, which in turn requires the work of mourning as the only means of resolving the psychic dilemma.

The Inca underlines the originality of Vitachuco's speech, but especially he wants to draw the reader's attention, toward the fact that the speaking subject is an Indian. In order to maintain the rhetorical argument, Garcilaso makes it clear that the words of the Indian rebel are conveyed to us through the messengers. For the first time in the text, we encounter the relationship between language and translation, which in turn involves the relation that exists between orality and writing, since the messengers communicated Vitacucho's words to us orally. Therefore, what reaches us is the legacy inherited by the reader consists of an artistic revision of the Renaissance model of writing with its conventions and rules in order to embellish the rhetorical dimension of speech, while also fulfilling the requirements establishes by Renaissance historiography. For this reason, the Inca emphasizes the exchange from the oral speech to the writing, anticipating the reflection upon the difficult task of narrating the events about the New World; and in particular, reveling the problem of representing the indigenous voices in a text that imitates the rules established by the discourse of Renaissance historiography. The act of writing is then the only available means of communication in the hermeneutic and expressive realms because it helps to interpret the American reality and to make it known to the European world. Through the figure of the translators, the Inca asserts his own status as an interpreter and mediator of different cultural codes. In this case, his self-representation is not elaborated and explained as it is done in other passages of the work, but still bears the burden of the limitations and dangers of his role. Such constrain are manifested as skepticism with regard to the possibility of giving reliable testimony, and for that reason the Inca makes use of rhetorical ornament to embellish the historical discourse, and also refers to the epic poems of Ariosto and Boiardo as literary models of Vitacucho. The direct allusion to Boiardo and Ariosto, places Vitacucho's speech within the prestigious literary tradition of epic poetry, where the hero's discourse constitutes one of the main topics since the origins of this genre. In his work, Garcilaso imitates this literary model in order to ascribe greatness nobility to his character. But why the direct reference to epic poetry instead of the chronicles of the conquest? It is not only for the prestige enjoyed by epic poetry. If we pay a closer attention to this issue, other reasons can be found that justifies the preference given to epic poetry over the chronicles in Garcilaso's text. First, the author did not use other models available to him for the creation of indigenous characters as Montezuma from Hernán Cortés' second letter, or Mayobanexio from the *Historia de la invención de las Indias* by Fernán Pérez de Oliva. Although, Oliva's work was unpublished until the 20th-century, Garcilaso was able to consult the manuscript in Cordova, since his friend Ambrosio Morales, was the nephew and editor of Oliva's *Works* in 1586.

Recent studies on Garcilaso's work focuses on *La Florida* and epic poetry, in particular *La Araucana* by Alonso de Ercilla, and *Elegías de varones ilustres de Indias* by Juan de Castellanos. According to Pupo-Walker, with respect to the meaning of the discourse as well as to the formal arrangement of the events narrated, the *Orlando Furioso* may have exercised a remote influence on many passages of *La Florida* (80). Garcilaso imitates the model of epic poetry in order to accentuate the greatness of his main character, thus establishing the importance of Vitacucho who appears side by side with the protagonists of the epic poems by Ariosto and Boiardo. A thorough reading of chapters 20 to 29 of the Second Book of *La Florida* confirms that the intertextual relationship between Garcilaso's work with the *Orlando Furioso* is only a matter of indirect influence which in turn is mediated by *La Araucana* as one of the most renowned epic poems of his time. In my opinion Vitacucho is modeled after the character of the Araucanian Galvarino, since they are both tragic heroes who immolate themselves. A brief comparison between the actions and declamatory speech of both Indian characters reveals that they have many traits in common. Vitacucho is a defeated hero, and his image remains with us as a powerful memory on the tragic of the conquest of America. In contrast with other natives such as Quigualtanqui who remained alive to curse Hernando de Soto's expedition, and is remembered for his courage (Rabasa 215); Vitacucho did not survived the conquest, since he died during the campaign. However, both Indians played an important function in the text: to speak for themselves in order to denounce the cruel practices of the conquest (Rabasa 214). Nevertheless, we can perceive certain differences between the two indigenous characters. I think that Vitacucho has a greater influence due to his violent death, while Quigualtanqui does not experienced an heroic way of dying which more easy fall into oblivion. The glory of Vitacucho rests on literature's ability to transform this Amerindian rebel into a symbol of resistance to the Spanish conquest of America. The character of Vitacucho exists in the future, while Quigualtanqui is portrayed as a figure from the past. Vitacucho experienced a heroic death because he died in battle fighting the Spaniards. It is precisely the violent death in combat under unusual circumstances which allows us to talk about the similarities that can be observed between the Amerindian characters of Vitacucho and Galvarino. First, Vitacucho's opening remarks addressed to the ambassadors sent by the other tribes are similar in their denunciatory tone to the speech delivered by the Araucanian Galvarino to the senate.

Galvarino's address gathers the feelings of rebellion of the Araucanian people, and is the most significant speech given in defense of Amerindian rights that appears in La Araucana (Triviños 113-34). On the other hand, Vitacucho withouth any weapon assaulted Hernando de Soto with his own hands. This impetuous act was unexpected by the Spaniards, and coincides with Galvarino's attack of a Spanish slave after his own hands were amputated in another remarkable gesture of courage. Galvarino is hanged by the Spanish authorities after falling in prison for the second time, at this moment the narration of events is interrupted by Ercilla's voice, who denounces the cruel execution of the Araucanian rebel. For his part, Vitacucho died with his body pierced by the swords of Spanish soldiers after his unsuccessful attempt to kill Hernando de Soto. The comparison between Vitacucho and Galvarino has an objective that transcends usual readings of consulting sources and reviewing literary influences. A thorough analysis of the representation of the native characters allows us to understand other salient aspects of Garcilaso's text that derve further examination. The Inca recurs to the epic tradition of aesthetization of war (Quint 5), in which the poet identifies the individual warriors by their names in order to assess the contribution of these heroic figures and inscribe their deeds into the collective memory for posterity. With the resources provided by epic poetry, the Inca was able to develop a model for representing the natives, and given the right to bear his own name when he perform a heroic deed. Garcilaso emulate the tradition of La Araucana by introducing in his text several battles scenes where particular attention is devoted to the individual efforts of the Amerindian characters. The story of Vitacucho reveals how the Inca uses the epic genre to create fictions and tropes that fulfill an expressive function: to write a history of the conquest of America in which we not only hear the voices of the winners, but also the voices of the vanquished, and the dead.

Hence that explains why Vitacucho's story and the author's complaint appear together in the same passage similar to what Ercilla does when he tells in *La Araucana* the story of Dido and Caupolicán in same canto. This procedure is followed in the cantos devoted to the figure of Galvarino, after which the story of Fitón is narrated. The history of Vitacucho is a complex account because it incorporates elements of the epic genre, the rhetoric tradition, and it is also a meditation on literature and death. The association that can be established between literature and death is demonstrated at two levels in the text. First, as an historical event since it is the narration of events of an expedition that took place many years ago. Second, at the philosophical level (Chang-Rodríguez 27-52) because it conceal a "deeper truth" (Rabasa 209): that is, the feeling of defeat of the conquered natives, and the work of mourning for their dead. The story of Vitacucho fulfills a relevant function in Garcilaso's text: the projection of the feeling of discontent left by the defeat of the Incas, which hindered the accomplishment of the heroic deed. Garcilaso makes evident the demand of an act of sacrifice in order to create a myth. This is the role assumed by the character of Vitacucho in the story of Hernando de Soto's expedition: to set an example against surrender and betrayal. The story of Vitacucho projected the sense of anticipation experienced by Garcilaso concerning the conquest of Peru, and was finally radicalized by the act of writing *La Florida*.

# CHAPTER 9

Reading the Specter in the Law: Colonialism and Culture in the *Royal Commentaries* (1609) by Inca Garcilaso de la Vega

At first glance looking into legal issues in the *Royal Commentaries* face a scarcity of works devoted to this topic. I should clarify that in this chapter I will focus on criminal law, such as violations of norms and sanctions in Andean society. Therefore, I will not refer to the institutions of public law, including the right of conquest in the Inca Empire, or the legal and political thought of Garcilaso, studied by James Fuerst in his excellent dissertation *Mestizo rhetoric: The political thought of the Inca Garcilaso de la Vega*. Most studies on the legal issues in the *Royal Commentaries* merely present negative interpretations, because legal scholars do not read Garcilaso's text, but rather give legal criticism about his work. It is necessary first to understand the central problem in the reception of Garcilaso's works within the discipline of law. Most of the legal arguments in the *Royal Commentaries* are from other disciplines and are based on Hermann Trimborn's ideas, an ethnologist that studied the development of the Andean law. I refer to his work "The Importance of Pre-Columbian America to the Comparative History of Law", and "Social classes in the Inca Empire." In his analysis, Trimborn rejected many of Garcilaso's ideas because they do not correspond with his theoretical proposal. Trimborn states that the legal institutions that appear in the *Royal Commentaries* fail to make a systemic model of law. Trimborn's main point of criticism of the *Royal Commentaries* is the fragmentation in descriptions of the legal system of the Incas, but this picture is explained by two factors: first, the inability to know all the legal institutions that existed in the Andean society, and second, the lack of an absolute correspondence between Andean and European law which is the reference model for Trimborn. This analytical method has the same limitations as the functionalist model developed by evolutionary concepts in the interpretation of legal institutions, which requires the existence of functions similar to the European benchmark. Trimborn actually built his theory of Inca law from a comparative approach with European law, particularly focusing on the medieval German legal categories. In other words, the world Trimborn presents has too many aspects that do not correspond with the European legal system, and he understands that difference as a lack of thoroughness. Trimborn was looking for a legal system with categories, and well-defined structures and functions to incorporate within his theoretical framework. This coincides with the interpretations of the theory of functionalism in law because according to its tenets the legal functions cannot exist without a systemic structure. The problem with this method of analysis is that if the categories, structures and legal functions described in the *Royal Commentaries* do not match the model, it is impossible to speak of the legal system. To Trimborn, Garcilaso gives a fragmented description of incomplete institutions and functions. This image minted by Trimborn is deficient, and because his prestige in Andean studies, such an interpretation has important negative consequences for the reception of Garcilaso's book by legal scholars. Among Trimborn's more important legacies is the creation of the image that the *Royal Commentaries* is somewhat incomplete and fragmentary. A careful reading of the Spanish and indigenous testimonies shows that there is not a work that can provide a systemic view of Inca law simply because it never existed as a self-contained system according to the functionalist model; even the more complete description of Inca law by Guaman Poma, analyzed by José Varallanos, or the text by the 16th-century Spanish jurist Polo Ondegardo do not respond to this model.

In my opinion, the real value of the *Royal Commentaries* is the vision of Inca law that is itself large and fragmented. This feature of the law, which some studies confuse with the lack of data or information, is a new aspect in Garcilaso's work and responds to an author's rhetorical strategy in the handling of the narrative. This strategy understands the description of legal institutions and their functions as random and biased, and more importantly, disassociates the Inca and European legal institutions. This model is based on Garcilaso's transatlantic intellectual project marked by a cultural complexity that moves between Europe and America. It can be understood as a dialogue with the European Renaissance as analyzed by Margarita Zamora, as *mestizaje andino*, as proposed by José A. Mazzotti to mention the presence of an oral subtext, and as a problematic relationship between history, memory and identity explored by Christian Fernández. In my opinion, the legal discourse in the *Royal Commentaries* employs the same narrative strategies mentioned throughout the book.Garcilaso compares Inca and Spanish law. Sometimes the comparisons are explicit, but in most cases they are implicit and require a reader's familiarity with the history of legal ideas. In the absence of a written text in the Andean world, Garcilaso uses oral traditions to organize his narrative. Specifically, the passages in which Garcilaso serves as a constructivist, as a creator of legal realities, are those in which the referent is the direct legal text of the *Siete Partidas*. In this case it appeals to the authority in the Spanish legal system, but I think this is a feature of other more important issues in the analysis of the Andean law and the relationship between writing and law. Garcilaso faces the difficulty of explaining an Andean oral law, when it considered the primacy of the written European law. This covers (from his personal experience with the litigation of his family) that the absence of a code or written law is an obstacle to the acceptance of the concept of law in Inca society. This idea is important because in Western societies there is a correlation between a written code of laws and the recognition of the existence of a legal order in society.To compensate for this lack of a code or written law, Garcilaso had the idea to use as a reference the Spanish legal system (with a long history of laws and codifications, expressed in several texts) in the description of institutions and to help explain their function. Garcilaso used a hermeneutic method of approximate translation of the content of the legal role, but as far as possible kept the cultural field and the standard case definition, and sometimes comparing the Spanish word to the appropriate indigenous term. This procedure reflects the difficulty of translating the oral Andean law through the filter of the Spanish alphabet, where many Andean institutions began to vanish after the conquest. This method seems to be determined by Garcilaso's discursive strategies in the *Royal Commentaries*, identified by Julio Ortega as the three discursive models: "the discourse of abundance, which creates a fertile version of forms and meaning, the discourse of deficiency, which contrasts with a defective vision ... and the virtual discourse, which projects an alternative vision and means to become a reality" (11). This explains why the model is necessarily a virtual model from a European perspective and, more importantly, shed light on the reason why this description of the law is necessarily an incomplete picture.

The virtual nature of legal ideas in the *Royal Commentaries* raises the question: what is the point of seeking a "pure" Inca law in the descriptions that appear in the work of Garcilaso? Perhaps it makes sense in terms rescuing the legal culture in the text, but there is no "pure" Inca law in the *Royal Commentaries* because the cultural mix is also a metaphor that builds the legal discourse, understood as an interpretation of the Andean legal universe. By using the Spanish law as a reference to explain Inca law, it is impossible to prevent this cultural mixture. In turn, the lack of knowledge of Inca legal culture prevents knowing in detail all the institutions, as commentators of European law understand it to be.Garcilaso's method indicates another important methodological problem in the study of Inca law; I refer to the difficulties of equating legal systems in different cultural practices. Recent work by anthropologist Terence D'Altroy draws attention to the need to be more cautious with statements on law, in particular the need to interpret the existence of a second penalty in certain crimes as a response to domination in the Andean region, and not as a development of the legal culture in Andean society.

The task of a legal readingof the *Royal Commentaries* lies in how to resolve the conflict between legal and empirical realitythat transcend simplification of epistemological problems, and especially how to analyze non-western legal cultures, thereby avoiding a misrepresentation of Andean culture in Garcilaso's text. I think this is the problem that will be faced by future studies on legal issues in the *Royal Commentaries*; there is a theoretical difficulty that appears from the pioneer book by historian Jorge Basadre, *Historia del Derecho Peruano* (1937), the work of specialists in legal anthropology like John Howland Rowe "Inca Culture at the Time of the Spanish Conquest" (1947), Sally Falk Moore's, *Power and Property in Inca Peru* (1958), and is present in Javier Vargas's, *Historia del Derecho Peruano* (1993), in which the analysis of Inca law only appears as the institutions mentioned by the Spanish and indigenous chroniclers, but in which the contribution of the *Royal Commentaries* does not receive the recognition it deserves.Garcilaso presents a vision of Inca law in which the institution of criminal law appears to be intimidating. Although he develops a rationale for it being a natural act that is born of the life cycle in Andean society, there are other possible readings. First, the explanation works as an idealization of the author, but from a legal point of view, the interpretation of Garcilaso is similar to the 16th-century Spanish legal doctrine on the deterrent function of punishment. In setting out the rule, Garcilaso is able to effectively unite the norm, the infraction and the sanction. The author himself offers in Book II, Chapter XIII an example to support his thesis: "that made the penalty of the law so severely, and men naturally love life and hate death, came to hate crime." At first reading, the interpretation of the criminal law appears equated with nature, as a continuation of the life cycle, but there are other issues from the standpoint of criminal law to be considered. The explanation denotes a relation with legal primacy in the social differences and not in the homogenization of society, in contradiction with the vision of Trimborn. For example, Garcilaso distinguished different degrees of strictness in criminal penalties. There is a distinction when he says we can see the sanctions based on authorship, distinguishing the crime according to the author, and especially in the analysis of the aggravating circumstances of the offense given by the author's social standing. Social position as understood by Garcilaso is the responsibility of the individual to the community. Garcilaso's ideas relate to subjects according to authority, said that the penalty was more severe if the offender was a judge or authority, but we should not dismiss this passage as an idealized vision of Inca society because it seems too closer to European legal subjectivity.

Following the analysis of criminal law in the *Royal Commentaries*, Garcilaso defines and discusses the kinds of crimes, which refer to acts against the state for their case and indicates the complexity of Andean social relations. The author also uses Spanish law to locate the most serious breaches of such regulations: crimes against the Sapa Inca. According to the hierarchy of social organization, Garcilaso defines crimes against the official forms of religion, distinguishing the legal from the religious interdictions, a situation clearly exposed when he explains the case of family law and marriage. For example, he distinguishes between the legal practices of marriages among the royal Inca family and the religious practices of marriage in Book 4, Chapter 9:

> It will be well to treat of the mode of marrying throughout all the kingdoms and provinces subject to the Yncas. It must be understood, then, that every year, or every two years, at a certain time, the king ordered all the young men and women of marriageable ages, who were of his family, to assemble in the city of Cuzco. The girls were from eighteen to twenty years of age, and the men twenty-four; and they were not permitted to marry earlier, because it was said that they ought to be of an age to better govern their houses and estates, and that if they married earlier their conduct would be like a child (Vega 186).

In explaining the marriage of the subaltern (Book 4, Chapter 8), Garcilaso speaks of a distinction that reflects a construction of both religious and legal institutions. In the first, polygamy was the custom of the king marrying his older sister, but these actions were justified by religion, so this was not actually the transgression of a religious rule. On the contrary, the marriage among brothers and sisters in subaltern social groups was considered a breach of a legal rule. In other words, the marriage of the population was monogamous according to a legal norm created by the ruling group, but was not an absolute religious injunction, because the ban did not extend to the Inca elite.In *La verdad y las formas jurídicas*, Michel Foucault did not include any examples from the *Royal Commentaries*. While known to have certain passages from Garcilaso's work, would not be limited to the classical Greeks and Germanic law. There is a quote from the *Royal Commentaries* that speaks directly to the liability of the witness in court, and is very close to Foucault's thesis. Garcilaso in Book II, Chapter III correctly explains the death penalty as a case of transgression of the model of truth imposed by the Sapa Inca:

> The witness was not usually guilty of falsehood, because these people, were very timid, and very religious in their idolatry, they knew well that, if their falsehood was discovered, they would be punished, frequently with death, if the offence was a grave one. This punishment was inflicted, not so much on account of the mischief that the falsehood might cause, as because the offender had lied to the Ynca, and disregarded the royal command, ordering that no lie should be told. The witness knew that to speak to any judge was to speak to the Ynca himself, whom they adored as God; and this was their chief reason for not telling lies (Vega 65).

Penal Law has a special definition of sanctions because for the theory of criminal law is necessary to define a range of penalties to apply the sanction. Garcilaso mentions the death penalty in Inca law, the rates of death penalty, and the punishment mechanism, which involves State as the executor of the sentence. The offenses that carry the death penalty include murder, robbery, incest, rape, adultery, desertion in time of war, and habitual laziness, among others. In some cases, Garcilaso distinguishes local sanctions and enforcement of sanctions by the local authorities but the individual's life seems to be ultimately in the hands of the Sapa Inca as the supreme authority of society.In a culture where we find varieties of legal offenses, we hopefully find corresponding penalties. This is another aspect presented by Garcilaso in his work. One of the most striking features of the *Royal Commentaries* is the detailed explanation of the crime, its causes, and the social sphere surrounding the incident. Within this intellectual project, the author develops his method explaining the difference between Spanish and Andean cultures. The repetition of examples and the various areas of life from which Garcilaso takes these cases leave no doubt that he places these cases under Inca law. In my opinion this is one of the most remarkable passage in the book. Although ravaged by the sanction of their broader impact than other individual sanctions, Garcilaso had an emotional distance in describing the case, and most importantly, prevented the transfer of the penalty of law to morality or religion. That is, he avoids interpreting this sanction from the perspective of Christianity or a system of European moral norms.Commenting on this issue, Garcilaso is also facing the most significant risk from the standpoint of the law. This is the risk assumed by any commentator on non-Western societies and can manifest itself in two ways: First, in the attempt to subordinate the legal system to the Western model, discarding what is different or unique from non-Western societies; and second, in assuming a universality that imposes a superficial generalization of legal institutions, ignoring the cultural diversities between these societies. To avoid a misinterpretation of the death penalty, Garcilaso describes the most important features and explains the differences in relation to other criminal penalties in Inca society. According to Garcilaso, in some cases death penalty also applied to the offender, their relatives, and their communities. Punishment also involved the destruction of all collective properties, including the vegetation and animal life of the area. As punishment with a highly symbolic significance, it impels the destruction of life of the offender and his environment, and hence the sterilization of the ground, as the culmination of the act of deprivation of life. The ultimate goal of the penalty was to remove from the collective memory these people. This death penalty was applied, according to Garcilaso, in cases of rebellions, rape of the sun virgins, and neglect in the service of the Sapa Inca. In Book IV, Chapter III Garcilaso explains an example of this penalty:

> But as it seemed to them but a slight punishment only to kill a man for so grave an offence as the violation of a virgin dedicated to the Sun, his god, and the father of his kings, the law directed that the wife, children, servants, and relatives of the delinquent should be put to death, as well as all the inhabitants of his village and all their flocks, without leaving a suckling nor a crying baby. The village was pulled down and the site strewn with stones, that the birth-place of so bad a son might for ever remain desolate and accursed, where no man nor even beast might rest in the future (Vega 179).

The explanation offered by Garcilaso is an example of identity between the legal subject and the territory of the offense that no longer exists at that time in the Spanish law. The vision that Garcilaso gives us is of a criminal law that does not distinguish between ownership and physical environment in the most serious crimes and therefore the penalty does not separate the individual author from collective responsibility, involving a equal penalty for both guilty and innocent alike. It is an important chapter that marks an interface between law and culture in the *Royal Commentaries*, because this institution is only a legal reason for being, according to cultural values violated by individual challenges of the most important rules of that society.This relationship between law and culture in the *Royal Commentaries* appears in the explanations on the sanction of the death penalty. But if the Incas were forced to maintain a system of sanctions, with their respective institutions for implementation, there are other questions that are beyond the scope of a reading that pays attention only to the formal legal aspects without taking into account the cultural elements. In other words, which cultural elements in Inca society createdsevere penalties, and more importantly: what were the cultural norms of this intimidating nature? The answer is not simple, and in my opinion requires a more careful analysis of the relationship between law and culture in the *Royal Commentaries*. Before answering these questions is an explanation quote offered by Garcilaso. He says:

> This was the law, but it was never put into execution, because no man ever transgressed it; for, the Indians of Peru were very fearful of breaking the laws, and kept them very carefully, especially those relating to their religion and their king. But if any one had broken this law, the sentence would have been literally executed without any remission whatever, as if it had been only a matter of killing a small dog. For the Yncas never made laws to frighten their vassals, but always with the intention of enforcing them on those who ventured to transgress it (Vega 180).

Garcilaso's words reveal that law cannot be seen in isolation from society. According to the quoted passage, the legal part of the culture and its specificity is given because it serves to establish order among different aspects, which in turn are interconnected by means of the law. Garcilaso's assertion that this sanction existed only as a virtual intimidation to maintain order in Incan society is very important. This idea, although expressing the idealized vision of the author, is similar to recent theoretical conceptualizations of the legal anthropologist Lawrence Rosen, who considered a more complex relationship between law and culture. According to Rosen, the law is an ordered lattice, which interconnects relationships with all elements of the cultural system of a society, and therefore if we cannot understand the concept of law, then we fail to understand the profound sense of order in the culture of that society. This also appears to be the subtext of the event mentioned in the *Royal Commentaries*, which could only be understood as a response to the rupture of culturally complex concepts linking politics, religion, and society. This punishment, Garcilaso says, exists as a material expression of cultural order established by the Sapa Incas, and cannot be misconstrued as an exercise for ineffective power, but as a manifestation of the violence of power ("to carry on those who dare to break") to maintain a sense of cultural order.

Most legal studies in the *Royal Commentaries* have omitted the cultural element of the law, reducing it to a set of rules and institutions established to govern populations and territories conquered by the Incas. This approach ignores that the law in Andean society was primarily a set of social practices organized to maintain order. Inca law was intended to meet broader cultural norms regarding how to exercise control over the subordinate populations. Thought and legal practice in Inca society was an exercise in domination. The most important conclusion in the *Royal Commentaries* is that the real vision of Andean legal culture can only be understood in all its complexity if we understand that the law is not only a formal, slightly reduced set of definitions, but a cultural product that has as main purpose: the imposition of principles of social control with the aim of dominating human groups. Violence cannot be understood separately from Inca law because the law depends on social practices of Inca dominance for their efficiency and performance. The law is incomplete without a practice of violence, hence, the justification of the violence of the law through cultural interpretations.

# CHAPTER 10

## The Afterlife of Colonial Legal Texts: Spanish Legal Imperialism and the Conquest of America

Legal norms are rhetorical strategies, designed to give an appearance of absolute truth. Therefore, the law is a narrative that attempts to abolish the distinction between reality and fiction. In this sense, the aim of this chapter is to study the legal procedures of Spain as legal fictions to justify the conquest of America. My point is that Spanish colonial legislation can only be understood in all its complexity by parting from the premise that the legal discourse is not just conceptual. That is, laws are not reducible to a set of abstract definitions, because the legal discourse itself is a discursive construction, whose metaphor is derived precisely from the need to disguise the purpose of imposing some principles of social control that are part of all legislative activity. In other words, the colonial laws of Spain in America must be studied not only as a set of rules or institutions, but as a discursive practice of imperial domination. This methodological approach is based on the idea that there is a link of complicity between the law and injustice in the conquest of America. To understand this apparent contradiction, it is necessary to consider the law from the perspective of postcolonial legal studies (Kumar 7-9). As Mendieta lucidly states:

> Already the Amerindians, the slaves of the New World, the *mestizos* and mulattos that are born with the modern project, knew in their flesh and sequestered and quarantined sociality what the postcolonial thinkers began to discover after the sixties and seventies in light of a process of decolonization begun in the aftermath of World War II (93).

First, the discursive status of legal thought offered the possibility of finding instances of struggles over ideas and practices surrounding the concepts of justice and rights. More simply, given the rhetorical nature of Spanish law in America, legal texts can be read as narratives of justification and resistance simultaneously. Most studies on the law only consider European legal texts as narratives of justification. They analyze only the legal text but do not take into account the context of political and social action of these texts because behind every law also exist unwritten laws that respond to the conventions, protocols and uses of power (Baxi, 2000: 540).The true history of law in colonial America is the story of an asymmetric inequality between oppression and resistance. The main paradox of the history of law in Latin America is the existence of sophisticated legal texts and debates at the time of a triumphant Spanish imperialism. The study of the development of colonial law not only reveals the unjust nature of the legal instruments of the conquest of America, but also allows for a critical review of the legal imperialist mentality that sought to introduce these laws and debate among the various schools of legal thought in Spain as charitable activities for Native Americans. Contrary to appearance, the results of this process reveals the complicity between European law and the mentality of imperial domination through a formal system of legal protection as part of sophisticated intellectual debates about the "human nature" of the Amerindian. The cultural construction of European identity was analyzed by Eve Darian-Smith and Peter Fitzpatrick:

> What is less remarked, and what initiates the defining moment of postcolonialism, is that the exclusion of these "others" is intrinsically antithetical to the West's arrogation of the universal to itself since this arrogation would require the inclusion within the West of those very others excluded in its constitution. The postcolonial –that is, the person subjected in this process- thus torn between exclusion as something radically different to the West and the demand to join and become the same as it (Darian-Smith and Fitzpatrick 1-2).

The main legacy of European law in Latin America was a colonial society masked by an assimilation/exclusion antinomy which is the philosophical foundation of the injustice of the conquest of America. The formal expression of this law was the "Laws of the Indies", which in practice were only a guide for governing colonies, they were orders to be fulfilled and no laws to articulate a defense of the rights of subordinates peoples. According to the medieval Castilian law that provides a legal basis for the Columbian expeditions, in which the dominance of the Catholic Monarchs over new territories is legitimate, one of his vassals had to take possession of the conquered lands (Seed 69). The legal institution that describes this ceremony is a concept which derives from Roman law and which retains its legal validity during the Conquest of America. Occupation is defined in the *Siete Partidas* and this method of acquiring property is tantamount to taking possession of something that does not belong to anyone, and that is designated *res nullius*, including the case of the *insula in mari cream* (the island that appears unexpectedly in the sea). In this situation the island is considered *res nullius*, it becomes the property of its first occupant. Since the land does not belong to anyone, the Kingdom who takes possession through the *Occupatio* acquires the right to his property, according to what is stated in the *Siete Partidas* (III 28). The key difference here is that it only refers to land uninhabited. In the tradition of Roman law and medieval Castilian law, it makes no reference in terms of the occupation of lands, except when there is a war. This is the special circumstance that allows us to understand why they resort to canon law to try to clarify the complex legal relationships that exist between the concepts of dominium and *possessio* regarding the territories of America.

As stipulated in medieval Castilian law, the Catholic Monarchs use Columbus as Admiral to conduct the occupation of the territories, an act which in turn gives the Monarchs symbolic possession of the land. Therefore, the occupation is the legal requirement to claim possession of new lands. Through Columbus, the Catholic Monarchs gain possession of the islands in the Caribbean. The Admiral exercises physical control over the occupied territories, which he seeks to consolidate through a small group of Spaniards housed at Fort *Navidad* and die in a battle against the Indians. The Santa Fe *Capitulaciones* of 1492 constitute the legal remedy used by the Catholic Monarchs to put their legal claim of possession (Kadir 65-76; Zamora 27-36). Referred to in this chapter as the right to hold disputed ownership of these territories within the framework of medieval Castilian law, it was designed to protect the Catholic Monarchs, since they used a representative to take possession in the absence of the true owner. Hence, in reality, the island's occupation by Columbus is a simple possession. As temporal measure, from a legal point of view the action requires the Admiral's legal recognition to establish legality.

In legal terms, the main aspect is to ascertain whether there is an *iusta cause possessionis*, as a legal title to legitimize the acquisition of these territories, and in turn establish who has legal dominion. This concept is derived from Roman law, which determines that the individual exercises a power over a corporeal thing, meaning the right of the owner to use and dispose of it freely. The right of the owner is called *re potestas* and gives him the power over a thing, because the owner has the power to dispose of his property and exclude others from using it (Marrero-Fente 2000: 93-99). At the time of the Columbian expedition, the provisions of Roman law are reinterpreted by canon law. The mediation of canon law is precisely in response to the rivalry between Spain and Portugal to gain control of the islands in the Atlantic Ocean. The changes introduced by canon law from 1436 with the Bull *Romanus Pontifex*, and several revisions until 1454, recognizes the Portuguese right to the Canary Islands. James Muldoon (105-10) and Robert A. Williams (59-66) have demonstrated the importance of this legal text, and both conclude that it is an example of the high sophisticated level reached by canon law. Muldoon locates this legal document in the context of a conflict for the Canary Islands that the King of Portugal Duarte I asked for a legal interpretation from the Pope Eugene IV in 1436. For its part, the letter prompted the actual written response from two prominent canonists of the time, Antonio Minucci and Antonio Roselli of Pratovecchio, who were commissioned directly from Pope Eugene IV. Despite the views of both canonists, the responses were not drafted as a direct reply to the letter of King Duarte I of Portugal, since his statements were only the basis of the argument offered by the Pope Eugene IV. More importantly, the letter established the legal basis for the conquest of territory outside Europe by the Christian kingdoms. Therefore, in certain circumstances, the Pope could authorize the invasion and occupation of these territories by Christian armies. In their explicit responses, both canonists maintained that the Pope was the only individual responsible for authorizing the conquest of the inhabitants of these territories as long as the conduct of the natives contradicted the principles of natural law (Muldoon 128; Williams 72). The relevance of the approaches formulated in the texts of Roselli and Minucci was that it was the basis for the legal framework that served as justification for other conquests. For the first time, canon law provided both a legal theory that neither Roman nor Castilian law could offer. The main thesis based on this legal doctrine is the relativity and finally denial of the dominium of the inhabitants of the conquered territories, together with the need to expand Christianity.

In a major study on the concept of *dominium* in political theory, James Burns highlights the trajectory of the concept during the Middle Ages. Burns argues that the idea of dominium never became a political term, but simply legal, which originated in Roman law, the philosophy of Aristotle and the patristic. To understand the concept of dominance in political discourse, it is important to consider two aspects: the first is of a legal nature, as the term is derived from the law and legal theory stating that property relations are based on the Roman law and the second explores the theological dimension of the concept. The two aspects are intertwined, so the new formulation of dominium in medieval political discourse demonstrates the greater the influence exerted by the jurists and theologians (Burns 16-29). The literature of the Middle Ages covers a number of works discussing the concept of dominion from the perspective of the divine and secular law. These medieval texts offer a synthesis around the ideas of the temporal and spiritual authority of the Pope, thus helping to establish a distinction between the spiritual and temporal sphere. It was from this division of powers that the term began to acquire a political connotation. According to Walter Ullmann, in medieval times, the supremacy of the Pope extended to the whole world, without taking into account religious beliefs, while the domain of the emperor was confined only to areas where Christianity prevailed (78). The thesis about universal domain requires a more detailed explanation when it comes to islands and seas. The complexity of the argument around the concept of medieval dominance over the islands and land is accepted by Weckmann, and refuted by García Gallo who rejected the idea of universal dominion on islands and territories. But if this debate is permeated by various interpretations of the legal doctrine, the confusion increases when the concept of dominium extends to the sea. Under the common law tradition that arose in medieval Europe, it is necessary to draw a distinction between control over land and dominion of the ocean. The law of the time recognized the possibility of territory as *res nullius*, which means that it does not belong to anyone. However, the Ocean was considered as *res communis* by Roman law.

Reacting to the intervention of King John II of Portugal to claim rights in the new lands founded by Columbus, the Catholic Monarchs appeal to Pope Alexander VI. The conflict between the two Iberian monarchies for the new territories in America cannot be resolved within the framework of Roman law, Castilian or Portuguese law. Hence, the dispute is submitted to the jurisdiction of canon law, and results in the bulls of Alexander VI in 1493, an act by which the Catholic Monarchs preserve their grip on the new American territories. Such action is illegal because it conflicts with what is stipulated in the European common law, which does not refer to the conquest of those territories which are inhabited, as referred to earlier in the case of the *Siete Partidas* (III 29). On the other hand, it lacks legitimacy in the absence of a consensus among the authorities, represented here by the Catholic Monarchs and the inhabitants of the conquered lands. In this case, the agreement reached in the legal documents of the Vatican is between parties who do not represent the people of America, and canon law doctrine prevails as in Africa and the Canary Islands. The legal outcome was more significant since the representation of the Amerindian is as a being devoid of legal personality within the scope of European law (Dussel 36-40; Subirats 407-63). Such a gesture of exclusion seeks to justify a history of clashes with the so-called infidels, and ideas that are spread around the inferiority of non-European peoples (Pagden 13-36). The novelty here is the move of the purview of the common European law to canon law to develop the argument in favor of the conquest of indigenous peoples, imposing the philosophical conception of natural law, from the doctrine of the decree of Gracian, and the Roman *ius commune*. The bulls were used to create the legal fiction of the monopoly of navigation and discovery in favor of the Catholic Monarchs (Marrero-Fente 2000: 99-122) and prepared the groundwork for the conquest. Since 1493 the conquest became a state enterprise, with the support of the Church.

This explains that according to the legal rhetoric of the text, the first element that is based on this act of aggression against the Amerindian is their conversion to Christianity. This company sets the pattern of the two paths of conversion to Christianity, the peaceful and military. It was this ambiguity in the discourse of canon law, which legally validated the existence of violence against Native Americans. The main consequence of the bulls of Alexander VI was that it facilitated the submission of the Amerindian peoples and their political domination. García Gallo explains that the legal precedent of the unbelievers did not apply in the case of America as the "apostolic authority actually appeared as a new set of essentially political issues. Only later would try to identify it with the fullness *potestatis* doctrine defended by Ostiense, but in the bulls of Alexander VI, there is nothing that allows such an identification" (664).In fact the Bulls of 1493 represent the beginning of a new mentality in which legal subjects are outside the legal discourse. The exclusion of the indigenous people of America from European law marks the opening of the American legal otherness, which arises from the colonial condition, inside/outside the law, a epistemological turn called coloniality of power (Mignolo 149-159; Quijano 215-32). The bulls of Alexander VI drew up a legal fiction to award to the Catholic Monarchs the political dominance of jurisdiction over those territories that were not part of the European legal doctrine. This action was not a single gesture, but rather part of a series of acts of aggression perpetrated since the fifteenth century against the African territories, as well as the Atlantic Ocean islands. The fundamental difference in the case of the bulls of 1493 is to justify future acts of aggression, which lays the foundations of legal doctrine dominating modern times: the grant given the Catholic Monarchs to advance possession of all the territories situated to the West of the demarcation line established by the bulls. This claim of universality *a priori* set out in European law serves as a justification in the conquest of America and subsequently to carry out the plans of aggression against Africa, Asia and Oceania since the sixteenth century.

The idea of universality was ultimately justified by the right of conquest, and reveals the European imperialism project against the peoples of Africa, America, and Asia. This Eurocentric nature of the right of conquest was the unwritten clause in all subsequent legal action. The first case in the practice of these ideas occurs in 1512 in the city of Burgos when a meeting convenes to discuss the "nature" of Native Americans. The meeting was chaired by Bishop Rodríguez de Fonseca, with the participation of lawyers Hernando de la Vega, Zapata, Mojica, Santiago De Sosa and Juan López de Palacios Rubio, and theologians Fray Tomas Durán, Fray Pedro de Covarrubias, and Friar Matías de Paz. The result of these sessions was a seven-point declaration that expressed the general ideas on the "treatment of Indians", but without offering concrete solutions to the conditions of conquest. The report also added a query to theologian Gregorio, and Fray Bernardo de Mesa, a Dominican priest, who supported the right of the Crown to submit the Amerindians (Morales 308). The first task of the *Junta* of Burgos was to find the solution to the legal conflicts of conquest in the European law. On December 27, 1512, the Royal Council enacted ordinances reaffirming Burgos's laws and the legitimacy of conquest based on the jurisprudence of the European *ius commune*.

The laws of Burgos are a summary of the European legal doctrine of conquest and colonization of non-European peoples. The most outstanding part this legal fiction is an introduction of legal instruments as laws in times of peace, which replaced the brutal practices of the military conquest. In fact, the laws of Burgos were a formal change of the legal discourse because there is no difference between these and the ultimate goals of the military doctrine of conquest. Burgos ordinances were adopted with the idea of legislating problems in times of peace but a peace that "appears to millions of people as forms of belligerency by other means" (Baxi 2002: vii) because they "produce human suffering in peacetime as in war-like situations" (Baxi 2002: vii) to justify slavery hidden in parcels of forced labor and the destruction and forced displacement of indigenous communities. The difference here is that the laws of Burgos try to hide the magnitude of physical violence and psychological operations that produce immeasurable human suffering. The complicity of the language of law creates the paradox as producer of injustice, where the language of rights is also "a factor of production of human suffering" (Baxi 2002: viii). The most important contradiction of the colonial legal system is that as soon as more laws appear in Burgos, Valladolid, Barcelona and Madrid, more Indians are deprived of their rights and oppressed by the *encomenderos*.

The laws of Burgos assume that the exercise of rights over indigenous people is legitimized through devices prescribed in the legal text, but the real ways of exercising these rights have an independent existence outside the law and its operation is impossible in a colonial society. These unwritten laws supersede the legal documents (Spivak 155-56) as the laws of Burgos, governing the treatment of the natives, but failed when they tried to be applied in a colonial reality, which by its very exploitative nature nullified any possibility of justice. Discussions on "fair titles" and "the nature of the Indians" by the *Junta* of Burgos in 1512 was a paternalistic action, based on the alleged social and cultural inferiority of indigenous people, and at worst served as an accomplice of Spanish imperialism in America.

Another problem that the *Junta* of Burgos attempted to resolve was the so-called "*justos títulos*," or the indisputable right of Spain to conquer the American territories. The solution was the *Requerimiento*, a legal instrument designed to meet the formality of law. This document was written by two members of the *Junta* of Burgos: the jurist, Juan López de Palacios Rubio, a professor at the University of Salamanca and adviser of the Catholic Monarchs, and the Dominican priest, Fray Matías de Paz, professor of theology at the University of Salamanca. The legal, theological and political requirements were outlined in the *Book of the Oceanic Islands* by Juan López de Palacios Rubio, and *Concerning the Rule of the Kings of Spain Over the Indians* by Matías de Paz which constitute the most elaborate defense of the Spanish right of conquest over the indigenous peoples of America. The *Requerimiento* was a written statement that was read aloud to the natives in order to subjugate them under the Kings of Spain. *The Requerimiento* is an order and therefore cannot be questioned by the natives. The formal structure of the text has five integrated parts explaining the creation of the world according to Christianity, the authority of the Pope of Rome, the act of donation of the bulls of Alexander VI, the mandate of evangelization, and finally the requirement of the Indians to recognize the monarchs of Spain as lords and kings of these territories (Morales 341, Pereña 36).

We cannot forget that the law in Latin America was used to subdue the indigenous to colonialism and these natives were incorporated into the imperial legal discourse. The paradox of the colonial law is that it originates in America, but this condition was also denied in the foundational fictions of European colonial law. It was the colonial experience in America that identified the development and improvement of standards and legal thought in Spain in order to subdue and control the American Indians. The strategy adopted by Spanish imperialism and this process of creating law and legal debates surrounding them were taken from Spain. Behind this argument lies the idea of the moral superiority of Europe, able even to consider "doubts" on the "nature" of the Amerindian. In reality these acts were a reaction to the natives response to the imperialist aggression. Indigenous testimonies are not retained and therefore the colonial legal history does not speak of these actions of resistance. Despite the few legal testimonies of indigenous people, one testimony appears in Martín Fernández de Enciso's, *Summa of Geography* published in Seville in 1519. This testimony presents the response of the cacique of Darien to the *Requerimiento*.

The words of the cacique of Darien function as a counter argument and a public confrontation of the brutality disguised as colonial law. The cacique of Darien states in the testimony cited by Bartolomé de las Casas:

> They replied that as far as saying that there was but one God and that this ruled heaven and earth and who was lord of all that seemed good, and that this should be so. But what he was saying that the Pope was lord of the whole universe, rather than God and that he had gave that land to the King of Castile, said the Pope must have been drunk when he did, because he gave what was not his, and that the King, who called and took the grant, must be some crazy, because what was asked of others. And it was there to take it, they will put their head on a stick, as were others who showed me of his enemies, ... and told me that they were lords of their own land, and had not needed another lord (Casas III 44-45).

The response of the cacique of Darien to the three main arguments of the *Requerimiento* is direct and uses a simple logic: they are actions of a "drunk" who "gave what was not his" and a "madman" who "asked what was belonging to me." For the cacique of Darien such actions are incomprehensible because they lack a basic reason, moreover, against the violence of military aggression he responds with the logic of resistance. The response of the cacique shows the accomplice role of European law in the justification of the unjustifiable: the imperialist aggression towards the Amerindian people. Studies on sixteenth century legal history discussed the violence of the conquest as a situation outside the Spanish law, and therefore try to exonerate the law from the violence, separating it from the actions of the conquerors. In fact, the Spanish law justified such practices of imperialist aggression, because the monarchy was acting as last ruler of justice. The greatest challenge of postcolonial interpretations of the law is to avoid reproducing the Eurocentric view that suggests that the "laws of the Indies" contained the possibility of "fair treatment" to the Amerindians. Despite the positive efforts of Bartolomé de las Casas and Francisco de Vitoria, none school of legal thought in early modern Europe came into doubt about the ontological superiority of Europe in which the colonial policy was implemented with the ruthlessness of imperialism in America.

The reality of colonialism destroythe possibility of justice because they were the same "laws of the Indies" which allowed the existence of slavery in the *Encomienda* system with the aftermath of abuse, oppression and suffering for millions of human beings. What is the main issue then is to rethink the debate on indigenous rights in the conquest of America in terms of the relationship between agency and method, and in particular to return to the key questions: who are we talking about and what injustice we will highlight?(Baxi 2002: xiii). From the viewpoint of indigenous people it does not matter much if this suffering and denial was based on religious considerations or legal advice. We must reverse the thinking to reject the imperialist mentality that justified that "the power of a few" becomes "the destiny of millions" (Baxi 2002: 25). So the work of restoring the violated rights of indigenous communities begins with the decolonization of colonial legal studies from an increased identification with indigenous cultures (Rabasa 83-84; Verdesio 35-48). The main task of the postcolonial legal studies is to analyze the logic of exclusion from European law in order to understand the destructive impact that the legal instruments had on the Amerindian societies and the consequences of those actions in the current indigenous communities of Latin America.

# CHAPTER 11

Human Rights and Academic Discourse: Teaching the Las Casas-
Sepúlveda Debate in the Times of the Iraq War.

The issue of human rights is above any political system and government; it is at the core of human society because it gives meaning to the concept of "human being" at its deepest dimension. Human rights place the individual at the center stage of thought and action—beyond politics, culture and economics—and condemn as intrinsically immoral any expression of discrimination or exclusion based on nationality, race, ethnicity, religion, gender, and sexual preference. It is imperative that we preserve the debate on human rights in our societies as the means to develop the full potential and integrity of every individual. However, the question remains as to how we can inscribe the State and its citizens and non-citizens alike within this framework of mutual respect, where individuals are protected from the excesses of the State (Weissbrodt 15–26). Obviously there continues to be a gap between the ideals proclaimed, the objectives declared, and reality itself. It is precisely within the university where human rights issues can be discussed and debated. And it is in our role as professors that we can promote among our students an academic culture based on the human values of solidarity and mutual respect.

On November 19, 1974, the United Nations Educational, Scientific, and Cultural Organization (UNESCO) promulgated a legal document of international scope, where the general guidelines concerning human rights where outlined for educational institutions. The guiding principles of this Declaration (the UNESCO Recommendation Concerning Education for International Understanding, Co-operation and Peace and Education Relating to Human Rights and Fundamental Freedoms, 1974), place education at the center of the human rights program. According to UNESCO, the educational policy regarding human rights should follow a global and multicultural perspective that aims to develop a sense of respect, solidarity, and cooperation between peoples and countries. From my perspective, the central tenet of the declaration is the repudiation of war as a solution to international conflicts that arise among nations. The declaration establishes that peaceful mentality is the main component of the human rights education program, and the best protection against all forms of aggressive behavior among States. In this context, we must explore the role of professors in the teaching of human rights in the classroom. The first question that must be raised is whether or not we may limit ourselves to a descriptive teaching of human rights. In agreement with Douzinas, I believe that if our duty is to educate, a descriptive approach is not appropriate (177–97). On the contrary, as professors we should neither assume an impartial position concerning human rights, nor must we apply a normative ethics (Dussel, *Etica* 25–32) that will allow us to describe and explain the differences between what is fair and what is unfair.

One of the most difficult tasks facing educators in my field is the negotiation between ancient texts and contemporary demands. This is the case of teaching Colonial Latin American texts that require waging a battle between medieval legal frameworks and modern concerns. Unfortunately, even as a myriad of strategies and approaches have been developed in the field of colonial studies, they have neglected to examine the corpus of laws as cultural production. Nevertheless, it is precisely critical legal theory that can provide an accessible medium for exploring the connection between law and violence. The omission of the cultural element in colonial studies reduces the complex *Laws of the Indies* to a mere set of rules or institutions implemented to govern the colonies. In other words, such an approach does not take into account that the Spanish legislation in America was primarily a set of organized social practices of violence, which served as a general guide prescribing what to do, what to seek, and how to exercise control over newly found people and their territories. In my view, legal thought and practice is at heart an exercise of human dominance. My point is that colonial legislation can be understood in its complexity only when it is understood that legal discourse is not merely conceptual—that is, not reducible to a set of definitions—but also a cultural product. As such, its metaphorical and associative quality derives precisely from the need to address the question of imposing principles of social control, which is at the center of any legislative controversy. In short, legal discourse is both cultural and normative in nature. Neither colonial legislation nor the violence it causes may be understood separately since colonial legislation is an incomplete practice without violence—it relies upon the social practice of human dominance for its efficacy.

For several years I have taught a seminar on Latin American literature and culture with an interdisciplinary approach to the study of the junctures of international law, human rights, and the international justice system in Latin America. The class introduces students to the legal systems of the region through the study of academic and specialized discourse pertaining to the humanities and the social sciences, combining historical, legal, philosophical, and political perspectives. Topics include the human rights movement in Latin America, the international body of law on human rights, and the international justice system with specific focus on selected human rights cases of the region. The violation of human rights in Latin America is a complex issue, which demands this kind of interdisciplinary approach in order to achieve a more holistic understanding of the social conflicts in the area. In this regard, the course examines the role of human rights organizations and locally-based groups and their connections with international institutions, governments, and non-governmental organizations. By outlining an understanding of the important conflicts and crises that mark the violation of human rights in Latin America, students gain a thorough understanding of development of the international law of human rights in the region, as well as its defense by lawyers, politicians, intellectuals and social movements. The seminar involves a review of substantive law through actual legal cases within their historical context. Besides reading legal documents, political texts and legislation, as well as reviewing the selected cases, students apply different theoretical approaches from the humanities and the social sciences. Requirements include preparation of assigned readings, presentation of analytical and comprehensive tasks, class discussions, case studies, exams, and a research project.

According to Mary Ann Glendon, one of the paradoxes in the history of the human rights movement is the pioneer role played by Latin America as a leader in the promotion of human rights in the United Nations, "in securing a place for human rights in the UN Charter, in providing models for the Human Rights Commission in its drafting process, and in endowing the UDHR with broad cross-cultural appeal" (39). The most important contribution of the region was the implementation of the legal procedures that made possible the enforcement of the rule of law. The unique position of Latin America in the international debate regarding the legal system of human rights constitutes a permanent legacy, and at the same time provided the means to fight against the violations of human rights by the military regimes during the 70s and 80s in the region.

As Paolo G. Carozzo has aptly proposed, "[t]he modern idea of human rights had a period of gestation lasting millennia. But it would be fair to say—even if it is not commonly recognized—that its birth was in the encounter between sixteenth century Spanish neo-scholasticism and the New World. If that encounter were embodied in a single person, it would be Bartolomé de Las Casas" (281). Based on that tradition, in my seminar I develop a model for teaching the paradigmatic positions of Bartolomé de Las Casas and Juan Ginés de Sepúlveda in their famous 1550 Valladolid debate regarding the Spanish war of conquest overseas, the nature of Amerindians and their rights to lordship and property, and the legality of European colonization. This model also allows for incorporating contemporary pressing issues such as the connection between international human rights law and the war in Iraq Students apply the same arguments and rhetorical structures of the sixteenth-century debate to the present and evaluate the lessons that can be learned from the past. The final objective is to incorporate debates on international human rights law in the classroom so students will understand that persuasion in its verbal or written forms is intricately linked to political thought and agency. In order to achieve a better understanding of the cultural background of the debate between Las Casas and Sepúlveda, students are divided into two groups, each representing the different perspectives of the debate. Both discussion groups are assigned a bibliography on the subject, and each team presents an opening statement on behalf of Las Casas or Sepúlveda. One of the students serves as moderator in order to maintain the rules and legal procedures of the debate.

From the readings and arguments that the students present, it becomes apparent that both Sepúlveda and Las Casas wanted the same thing: the conversion of the Amerindians. However, they wanted to achieve this in very different ways; their suggested methods were quite distinct. Las Casas was a proponent of a peaceful approach to conversion, while Sepúlveda believed in a violent method that would force the conversion of the Amerindians. Both sides used the Bible to support their arguments, and they also used sources such as Aristotle and other classical thinkers. As Santa Arias recognizes, Las Casas's writings on the conquest and the natural rights of the Amerindian provide unique insight into sixteenth-century European political culture, especially regarding concerns of history, political discourse, and power (121).

From my perspective, the single most important contribution of Las Casas was to frame the legal foundation of the human rights movement in Latin America. At the center of his intellectual agenda was the defense of the indigenous population in Latin America. As Mariscal maintains, "[o]ne of the characteristics that marked the ethical core of Las Casas's entire career was the militancy with which he confronted his adversaries" (260). In this sense, his fight marked the direction of the legal battles against social injustice in the future. The reasoning behind waging war against the Amerindians, according to Sepúlveda, was that they had an underdeveloped culture and they were born to obey and serve others like the beasts that they resembled (Hanke 63). He felt that it was necessary to take action in order to "liberate" them from this barbarous condition. His working definition of barbarism was based on the writings of Aristotle, who stated that barbarians were those who: 1) Display savage behavior; 2) Have no written language in which to express themselves; 3) Have an evil and wicked character; 4) Practice a false religion; 5) Lack the reasoning abilities and way of life suited to human beings; and 6) Lack laws which might regulate their affairs. The Amerindians were known for their religious sacrifices, which the Spaniards understood as the killing of innocent people. These barbaric acts went against the natural law of the Spaniards, and naturally categorized the Indians as savage beasts who needed to be conquered. Another of Sepúlveda's main arguments was that the Amerindians committed crimes against natural law, to which all humans are subject. As Alvira and Cruz point out: "Sepúlveda held up natural law as an absolute limit to the variations permissible among the different forms of human life. But when confronted with the fact that the Indians did not obey this law, he did not deduce that the law itself might not be so natural; he did not imagine that it could have been conceived according to cultural parameters" (105). Natural law is a broad concept, but basically refers to generally accepted human activities. Unacceptable activity would include human sacrifice and live burial, both of which the Amerindians practiced extensively. Sepúlveda was appalled at these "savage" acts, especially since he viewed them as a victimization of innocent members of the community. It is precisely in the natural law doctrine where we find one of Las Casa's more vigorous defenses of the indigenous population. Carozzo maintains that while Las Casas's ideas were intellectually and morally grounded in the Thomist tradition, his deployment of the discourse of the natural rights of the Indians was an anomaly in his time. Furthermore, by connecting abstract theories to real-life issues, Las Casas's pragmatic approach would go on to influence future theorizations of natural rights (292). But as Beuchot explains: "Although Las Casas never talked of human rights, his defense of the natural law and the law of peoples was also a defense of human rights" (53).

Other unnatural crimes Sepúlveda accused the Indians of committing were idolatry and sodomy. Sepúlveda viewed nearly the entire Amerindian lifestyle as unnatural in the eyes of God and nature, and therefore the Spanish were justified in setting them right—even by force and violence. An additional argument that Sepúlveda made to justify the intervention against the Amerindians was that they oppressed and then killed innocent people in order to sacrifice them to their gods or to eat their bodies. He explained that this only further displayed their animalistic and inhumane behavior. In order to show them the correct way of behaving and how to appropriately treat their fellow human beings, the Spanish needed to teach them Christianity. Sepúlveda's final argument for the justification of war as a lawful way of spreading Christianity in the Americas was that the Amerindians were infidels, who must first be conquered before they can be Christianized. To him, war was a necessary preparation for "preaching the faith." He based his argument on a biblical parable where God ordered his followers to scan the area and "force them to come in" and celebrate a wedding feast with the Lord's followers. This text demonstrates that the Lord has prohibited such use of force, if deemed a necessary precursor to rightly introduce the goodness of God to the infidels.

Bartolomé de las Casas believed that there was no race in the world, however rude, uncultivated, barbarous, or almost brutal they may be, that could not be persuaded and brought to a good order and way of life. According to Las Casas, "[a]ll the races of the world are men, and of all men and of each individual there is but one definition, and this is that they are rational. All have understanding and will and free choice, as all are made in the image and likeness of God [. . .]. Thus the entire human race is one" (*Apologética Historia* 165–66). All men are alike with respect to their creation and the things of nature, and none is born already taught. And so we all have need, from the beginning, of guidance and assistance from those who have come before us. He also believed that all the races of the world have understanding and will, which results from free choice. Consequently, all men have the power and ability or capacity to be instructed, persuaded, and attracted to order, reason, laws, virtue and goodness. Contrary to Sepúlveda, Las Casas proposed a method in which the "pagan" would first be subjected, whether they wished to be or not, to the rule of Christian people, and once subjected, organized preaching would follow (Pennington 149–50). His logic was as follows: if the "pagan" was first injured, oppressed, saddened, or afflicted by the misfortunes of war, through the loss of their children, their gods, and their own liberty, how could they be moved voluntarily to listen to what is proposed to them about faith, religion, justice, and truth?

According to Las Casas the one and only method of teaching men the true religion was established by Divine Providence for the whole world, and for all times: that is, by persuading understanding through reasons and by gently attracting or exhorting God's will. Like Augustine, Las Casas believed that Divine Wisdom moves rational creatures, that is, men, to their actions, and that it operates gently. Therefore, the method of teaching men the true religion ought to be gentle, enticing, and pleasant. Listeners, especially "pagans" should understand that the preachers of the faith have no intention of acquiring power over them. Preachers should be so mild and humble, courteous and good-willed that the listeners would eagerly wish to listen and hold their teaching in greater reverence. Las Casas gave a detailed rebuttal of each of Sepúlveda's arguments, beginning with Sepúlveda's statement that Indians are barbarous. Sepúlveda believed that since the Indians displayed barbarous tendencies, they were natural slaves and the Spanish had the right to claim superiority. This broad statement made it easy for Las Casas to defend the Indian; he examined the three facets of Aristotle's definition of barbarism which included savage behavior and a lack of a written language. In his explanation he demonstrated how this declaration of the Indians as savages was untrue, and therefore did provide sufficient reason for Spanish domination of the Indians. Las Casas easily rebuts the first two statements by showing how the Spanish also commit barbarous behavior in their treatment of the Amerindian, and how the indigenous language had been described as beautiful and intricate by some scholars. Regarding the last issue, which states that one is a barbarian if one has no laws and acts similarly to animals, Las Casas explained that no one race could be deemed insufficient because God had created all men. Therefore, this third statement does not apply to the Amerindian population. Las Casas spoke very highly of the Amerindian culture, while pointing out areas in which the Christians may be perceived as barbarians through their violent acts.

In response to Sepúlveda's argument that war against the Amerindian may be justified as punishment for the crimes they commit against natural law, Las Casas made several key rebuttals. First, Las Casas noted that "punishment presupposes jurisdiction over the person receiving it, but Spaniards enjoy no jurisdiction over the Amerindians, and hence they cannot punish them" (Hanke 87). He then continued to explain that people who profess a faith other than Christianity but live in a Christian kingdom are under jurisdiction of the Christian prince of that kingdom, but not concerning spiritual matters. More specifically, he goes on to argue, "Jews, Muslims, and idolaters who do not live in a Christian kingdom are not under jurisdiction of the church" (Hanke 88). This is clearly the case in the New World given that prior to its conquest, the people had never heard the teachings of Christianity, and thus were even less sinful than Jews and Muslims in the Christian perspective, who had heard the teachings of Christianity, yet still chose to practice their own beliefs. Finally, Las Casas claimed that the violence forced upon the Amerindians by the preaching of Christianity had been "contrived by the devil in order to prevent salvation of men and the spread of true religion" (Hanke 89). Christians did not have a right to engage in war based on the act of sacrifice and this long-standing practice is not to be "up-rooted" overnight. Las Casas also contested Sepúlveda's third argument claiming that Amerindians oppressed and killed innocent peoples. Sepúlveda justified the Spaniards' killing of Amerindians by the fact that the Amerindians killed innocent people for sacrifices. On the other hand, Las Casas said that "the Indians did not commit such acts, and that, if they did worship idols or engage in human sacrifices to their gods, these acts could be justified" (Hanke 89). First, Las Casas maintained that any man who would be willing to die for his own god should be honored. If his sacrifice is wrong in the eyes of God, then God will punish him. Las Casas also argued that Christian men are obligated to help others who are being harmed. This aid to people in danger should never result in moving against a multitude. This was the case of the Spaniards. The gospel instructs Christians to "preach the word to the nations;" however, "what does the gospel have to do with armed thieves?" (Hanke 91). Christians are not supposed to force their religion on others, especially in a violent manner.

The position of Sepúlveda is once again reinforced by his fourth argument, that "war may be waged against infidels in order to prepare the way for preaching the faith" (Hanke 95). Las Casas had many responses to this, although Sepúlveda even attested that the Bible supported his argument in the parable of the wedding. Las Casas refuted this by summarizing Sepúlveda's argument: "the gospel (which is the good and joyful news) and the forgiveness of sins should be proclaimed with arms and bombardments, by subjecting a nation with armed militia and pursuing it with the force of war" (Hanke 96). The contrast articulated here by Las Casas speaks volumes on the hypocrisy of Sepúlveda's biblical reference and is a powerful statement. Las Casas reminded his listeners of the words of Saint Paul: "Treat each other in the same friendly way as Christ treated you" (Hanke 96). The forcing of religion on pagans is not the Christian way; Las Casas recognized this and pointed out that Christ never advocated torturing the nonbelievers. The horrid maltreatment of Amerindians to convert them, to the way of Christ's love is illogical. Las Casas's last (and perhaps most tangible) rebuttal of Sepúlveda referenced the use of force by the Romans to gain their empire and convert the world to Christianity. Las Casas argued that the words of Augustine and Thomas Aquinas had been twisted by Sepúlveda to his advantage and that in no way does the despotism of the Romans at the height of their reign validate the use of cruel treatment toward the Amerindians. Las Casas showed that the Roman Empire no longer exists because God has punished it for its malicious actions, and Spain should by no means follow its example, for it too will perish. In this manner, Las Casas refuted the argument that war is justifiable to spread Christianity. Eduardo Andújar has pointed out the "colonialist mentality" of Las Casas's, stating that the Lascasian perspective was "affirmative and to some extent optimist," but with some limitations (84). Las Casas considered the conquest and colonization of Latin America a factual reality that had to be accepted by the indigenous population of the region. His fight with the Crown was to revise the interpretation of the conquest, but not to question the presence of the Spanish Empire in the New World. Another point made by Andújar is that the insistence on religious conversion was the central tenet of his intellectual endeavor. This point is the negative element of Lascasian thought, which marks another kind of violence, one that anticipated modern forms of colonial domination. Andújar's legal criticism to Las Casas is similar to Enrique Dussel's philosophical theory of the Other. Based on some of the arguments developed by Las Casas, Dussel elaborated on the category of the Other in his analysis of the conquest of America. He concluded that for Las Casas the inhabitants of the Americas constituted the Other, "a rustic mass discovered in order to be civilized by the European being (ser) of occidental culture. But this Other is in fact covered over (encubierto) in its alterity" (*Invention* 36). Dussel's argument rests on the notion that the Other is a socio-historical subject, since it is related to a particular period of time and to a specific geographical space. Dussel goes on to argue that the economic elements permeate all the relations between individuals in a society, and for that reason the Amerindian as the Other cannot be fully conceptualized outside the economic system. According to Mignolo, Dussel's position coincides more with a "Geopolitics of Christianity" similar to the Amerindian movement in Latin America than with any Eurocentric ideology (178).

But what are the connections between the Las Casas-Sepúlveda debate and the Iraq War? For Carozzo, Las Casas's ideas are at the foundation of the Latin American human rights tradition and are as applicable today as they were 400 years ago, since most of the indigenous population in Latin America is still searching for legal rights and human dignity. Carozzo also reminds us that while today's reader can identify elements of twentieth- century human rights discourse in Las Casas's sixteenth-century texts, this recognition has been criticized as anachronistic. However, he offers compelling reasons to include Las Casas in the trajectory of the development of human rights, particularly Las Casa's ability to recognize cultural integrity and self-determination as central elements in the rights of the Amerindians (295–296). In this sense, we should not read Las Casas's writings only as part of a distant past but also as a permanent contribution to the struggles for a better world and more just society. The progressive elements in Las Casas's thinking have become a central component in the human rights movement, and in particular in the peace movement against the war in Iraq. There are many interesting connections between Las Casas and Sepúlveda's debate and the ongoing war in Iraq. First, it is clear that the debate offered by Las Casas is much more humanistic in nature and is structured around four main arguments that have been discussed earlier. There are however several commonalities between these two cases. The greatest concern of Las Casas was the inhumane treatment and killing of a group of people he considers to be victims (Pereña 109–110). Since the U.S. invaded Iraq in 2003, thousands of innocent Iraqi civilians have been killed and even more have been mistreated. Take for example the Iraqi prisoner abuse scandal at Abu Grahib. Like Sepúlveda who reduced the status of the Amerindian to "beast and fierce animals whom they resemble" (Hanke 63), U.S. soldiers viewed Iraqi prisoners as animals and abused them not only physically, but sexually and mentally as well.

Another parallel can be drawn between the false pretenses of justification in both of these situations. The Spanish used the mask of religion to justify their conquest of America and its inhabitants, whereas the U.S. claimed to be ridding the world of a terrorist regime with Weapons of Mass Destruction, which ironically, were never found. But were Christianity and global security the real motives behind both of these invasions? Or were riches, territory and oil the real driving factors? We will never know the answer, but we do have our suspicions, and these suspicions, unlike the causes for invading these territories, are indeed justified.

As the Spanish tried to impose their faith and did so through cruel and inhumane tactics, so too is the U.S. trying to impose a western tradition and "spread democracy." In both cases, these societies are seen as inferior societies that must be in one case, saved through Christianity, and in the other, saved from a tyrannical ruler. What is important though are the mechanisms used by both the Spanish in the 1500's and the U.S. today, in order to "save" and "protect" these people. While Las Casas firmly denounced the violence and aggression by the Spanish, Sepúlveda stood by the actions of the conquerors and supports their involvement in armed conflict. George Bush viewed Saddam Hussein as a barbaric ruler that had to be taken out using any necessary means of force, and while Saddam is no longer in power, the Iraqi people have suffered and continue to suffer as a result of the violence that occurs on daily basis. Did "Operation Iraqi Freedom" really free the people of Iraq taking into consideration that in both of these cases, violence is the main mechanism used to "save" these people? While the U.S. claims to be winning the war in Iraq and the *encomienda* system was finally abolished in Spanish America, as a result of the unlawful deaths and the inhumane treatments inflicted upon both the Iraqi and Amerindian people, neither the U.S. nor Spain can be seen as successful in their respective endeavors. The lessons from the Las Casas-Sepúlveda debate and the war in Iraq are similar: the respect for human rights is the principal component in the relations among nations and its peoples.

Returning now to the classroom, in pedagogical terms the exercise on the Las Casas-Sepúlveda debate reveals another dimension to the students: the fact that one of the main causes of recent confrontation among States is the failure of politicians to promote the dialogue and exchange of ideas. In the course, I try to enhance cultural understanding by helping students develop the ability to reflect about Latin America. My primary role as a teacher of Latin American literature and culture is to help students be open to new ideas, and to enhance an appreciation of the differences in the customs, beliefs, and value systems of others. My goal is to promote an intercultural dialogue by motivating students to become aware of contrasts and similarities between their own culture and Latin American culture. I use an interactive teaching style in which students become active rather than passive participants in the learning process. Therefore, I try to create conditions in the classroom that promote active involvement between myself as a teacher and my students, and among students themselves. The benefits of utilizing this interactive teaching style is that it helps students to function both independently and in a team, while providing them with a chance to develop critical thinking skills that will enable them to engage in the class discussions as active thinkers rather than passive consumer of ideas. I incorporate the role of debate in the classroom in order to encourage students to focus in greater depth on a selected topic, while providing them with an opportunity to develop critical thinking skills and increase their motivation for future learning.

One of the lessons from the war in Iraq that is pertinent to our students is that we must begin to understand the roots of the aggressive mentality that prevails in our society. In that sense, the debate is not a futile exercise in argumentation, but a more relevant activity, in fact a fundamental component of any educational program, because it trains individuals to discuss their government's actions and the consequences. I believe that the debate should address not only today's crisis, but also the foundations of society including the patterns of aggression and the causes of violence. In that sense, we need to devote more attention to the ways in which communities create the actual conditions for aggression and violence in everyday life. The debate is not only an antidote to war, but it is also a good exercise in social responsibility that can replace both physical and mental violence. Teaching individuals in advance how to exchange different ideas and points of view is the best strategy to avoid a war. To promote dialogue among individuals is the first step to create a better world where there is no war and confrontation disappears. In today's world, international relations are based on the respect of international law (Coicaud, Doyle, and Gardner, 1–22), and the international criminal justice system as the foundations for global human security.

# BIBLIOGRAPHY

Abellán, José Luis. *Historia crítica del pensamiento español*. Madrid: Espasa-Calpe, 1979. Vol. 2. 155-57.

Abraham, Nicolas and Maria Torok. *The Shell and the Kernel: Renewals of Psychoanalysis*. Trans Nicholas Rand. Chicago: University of Chicago Press, 1994.

Agamben, Giorgio. *Stanzas. World and Phantasm in Western Culture*. Trans. Ronald L. Martinez. Minneapolis and London: University of Minnesota Press, 1993.

Aldunate del Solar, Carlos. *Cultura mapuche*. Santiago de Chile: Ministerio de Educación, 1986.

Alvira, Rafael, and Alfredo Cruz. "The Controversy Between Las Casas and Sepúlveda at Valladolid." *Hispanic Philosophy in the Age of Discovery*. Ed. Kevin White. Washington, D.C.: The Catholic University of America Press, 1997. 88–112.

Andújar, Eduardo. "Bartolomé de Las Casas and Juan Ginés de Sepúlveda: Moral Theology versus Political Philosophy." *Hispanic Philosophy in the Age of Discovery*. Ed. Kevin White. Washington, D.C.: The Catholic University of America Press, 1997. 69–87.

Arellano, Ignacio. "Problemas en la interpretación y anotación en las crónicas de Indias." *Edición y anotación de textos coloniales hispanoamericanos*. Ed. Ignacio Arellano y J.A. Rodríguez Garrido. Madrid: Iberoamericana, 1999. 45-74.

Arellano, Ignacio and Victoriano Roncero, *Poesía satírica y burlesca de los siglos de oro*. Madrid: Editorial Espasa Calpe, S.A., 2002.

Arias, Santa. *Retórica, historia y polémica: Bartolomé de las Casas y la tradición intelectual renacentista*. Lanham [Md.]: University Press of America, 2001.

Avalle-Arce, Juan Bautista. *La épica colonial*. Pamplona: Eunsa, 2000.

Baranda, Consolación. "De Pérez de Oliva a Cervantes de Salazar: Homenaje y tradición." Insula, 674 (2003): 22-25.

Basadre, Jorge. *Historia del derecho peruano*. Lima: Editorial Antena, 1937.

Baxi, Uprenda. *The Future of Human Rights*. New Delhi: Oxford University Press, 2002.

___. "Postcolonial legality." *A Companion to Postcolonial Studies*. Eds. Henry Schwarz and Sangeeta Ray. Malden, MA; Oxford: Blackwell, 2000. 540-55.

Beissinger, Margaret, Jane Tylus, and Susanne Wofford, eds. *Epic Traditions in the Contemporary World. The Poetics of Community*. Berkeley: University of California Press, 1999.

Beuchot, Mauricio. *Los fundamentos de los derechos humanos en Bartolomé de las Casas*. Barcelona: Anthropos, 1994.

Boccaccio, Giovanni. *Genealogía de los dioses paganos*. Madrid: Editora Nacional, 1983.

Burns, J. H. *Lordship, Kingship, and Empire: The Idea of Monarchy, 1400-1525*. Oxford: Clarendon Press, 1992.

Buse, Peter and Andrew Stott, eds. *Ghosts. Deconstruction. Psychoanalysis. History*. London: MacMillan Press, 1999.

Busto Duthurburu, José A. del. *La conquista del Perú*. Lima: Librería Studium, 1988.

Caravaggio, Giovanni. *Studi sull' epica ispanica del Rinascimento*. Pisa: Universitá di Pisa, 1974.

Carozzo, Paolo. "From Conquest to Constitutions: The Latin American Tradition of Idea of Human Rights." *Human Rights Quarterly* 25.2 (2003): 281-314.

Casas, Bartolomé de las. "Apologética historia." *Obras escogidas*. Madrid: Atlas, 1957–1958. 165–66. Vol. 3

____. *Historia de las Indias*. Ed. Agustín Millares Carlo. México: Fondo de Cultura Económica, 1951.

Castellanos, Juan de. *Elegías ilustres de Indias*. Ed. Isaac Pardo. Caracas: Academia Nacional de la Historia, 1987.

Cátedra, Pedro M. Ed. Enrique de Villena, *Traducción y glosas a la Eneida.* Salamanca: Biblioteca Española del Siglo XV, Diputación de Salamanca, 1989-1990.

___. *La historiografía en verso en la época de los Reyes Católicos. Juan Barba y su "Consolatoria de Castilla."* Salamanca: Universidad de Salamanca, 1989.

Cerrón Puga, María Luisa. "Fernán Pérez de Oliva traductor de Pedro Mártir de Anglería: *La historia de la invención de las Yndias.*" *Edad de Oro* 10 (1991): 33-51.

Certeau, Michel de. *The Writing of History*. Trans. Tom Conley. New York: Columbia University Press, 1988.

Chang-Rodríguez, Raquel. "Sobre la vertiente filosófica de *La Florida* del Inca." *Violencia y subversión en la prosa colonial Hispanoamericana, siglos XVI, XVII*. México: Literal Books, 1994. 27-52.

Clayton, Lawrence A., Vernon J. Knight, Edward Moore, Eds. *The De Soto Chronicles. The Expedition of Hernando de Soto to North America in 1539-1543*. Tuscaloosa & London: The University of Alabama Press, 1993. Vol. 1.

Coello, Óscar. *Los inicios de la poesía castellana en el Perú. Fuentes, estudio crítico y textos*. Lima: Pontificia Universidad Católica del Perú, 2001.

Coicaud, Jean-Marc, Michael W. Doyle, and Anne-Marie Gardner, eds. *The Globalization of Human Rights*. New York: United Nations University Press, 2003.

Colón, Hernando. *Historia del Almirante*. Ed. Manuel Carrera Díaz. Barcelona: Ariel, 2003.

Cortés, Hernán. *Cartas de relación*. Ed. Angel Delgado. Madrid: Castalia, 1993.

Curtius, Ernst Robert. *Literatura europea y Edad Media Latina*. México: FCE, 1955. 2 vols.

D'Altroy, Terence N. *The Incas. The peoples of America*. Malden, Mass: Blackwell, 2002.

Darian-Smith, Eve and Peter Fitzpatrick. *Laws of the Postcolonial. Law, meaning, and violence*. Ann Arbor: University of Michigan Press, 1999.

Davis, Elizabeth. *Myth and Identity in the Epic of Imperial Spain*. Columbia: University of Missouri Press, 2000.

Derderian, Katherine. *Leaving Words to Remember: Greek Mourning and the Advent of Literacy*. Leiden/Boston: Brill, 2001.

Derrida, Jacques. *Work of Mourning*. Chicago: University of Chicago Press, 2001.

___. *Specters of Marx: The State of the Debt, the Work of Mourning, and the New International*. Trans. Peggy Kamuf. New York and London: Routledge, 1994.

___. "Force of Law: the "Mystical Foundation of Authority." *Deconstruction and the Possibility of Justice*. Eds. Drucilla Cornell, Michel Rosenfeld and David Carlson. New York: Routledge, 1992. 3-67.

Deyermond, Alan D. "La historiografía trastamara: ¿una cuarentena de obras perdidas?" *Estudios en homenaje a don Claudio Sánchez Albornoz en su 90 cumpleaños*. Buenos Aires: Facultad de Filosofía y Letras, 1986. 161-193. Vol. 4.

Díaz del Castillo, Bernal. *Historia verdadera de la conquista de la Nueva España*. Madrid: Espasa, 1985.

Díaz Jimeno, Felipe. *Hado y Fortuna en la España del siglo XVI*. Madrid: Fundación Universitaria Española, 1987.

Dorantes, Baltasar. *Sumaria relación de las cosas de la Nueva España*. México: Porrúa, 1987.

Dougherty, Carol. *The Raft of Odysseus. The Ethnographic Imagination of Homer's Odyssey*. Oxford: Oxford University Press, 2001.

Douzinas, Costas. *Human Rights and Empire: The Political Philosophy Cosmopolitanism*. London: Routledge, 2007.

Dowling, Lee. "*La Florida* del Inca: Garcilaso's Literary Sources." *The Hernando deSoto Expedition. History, Historiography, and "Discovery" in the Sotheast.* Ed. Patricia Galloway.Lincoln & London: University of Nebraska Press, 1997.

Dowling Desmadryl, Jorge. *Religión, chamamismo y mitología mapuche.* Santiago de Chile:Editorial Universitaria, 1973.

Dussel, Enrique. *The Invention of the Americas: Eclipse of "the Other" and the Myth of Modernity.* New York: Continuum, 1995.

Eng, David and David Kazanjian, eds. *Loss: the Politics of Mourning.* Berkeley: University of California, 2003.

Ercilla, Alonso de. *La Araucana.* Ed. Isaías Lerner. Madrid: Cátedra, 1993.

Fanthan, Elaine. "The Role of Lament in the Growth of Roman Epic." InBeissinger, Tylus, and Wofford.221-236.

Faron. Louis C. *The Mapuche Indians of Chile.*Prospect Heights, IL: Waveland Press, 1986.

Fernández, Christian. *Inca Garcilaso, imaginación, memoria e identidad.* Lima: Universidad Nacional Mayor de San Marcos, 2004.

Ferreras, Jacqueline. *Les dialogues espagnols du XVIeme siècle, ou l'expression littéraire d'une nouvelle conscience.* Paris: Université de Lille, 1985. 2 vols.

Foucault, Michel. *La verdad y las formas jurídicas.* Barcelona: Gedisa, 1992.

Frankl, Victor. "Hernán Cortés y la tradición de las *Siete Partidas.*" *Revista de Historia de América* 53-54 (1962): 9-74.

Frye, Northrop. *Myth and Metaphor. Selected Essays, 1974-1988.* Ed. R. Denham. Charlottesville, Virginia: University of Virginia Press, 1990.

Fuerst James. *Mestizo Rhetoric: The Political Thought of El Inca Garcilaso de la Vega.* Ph.D Dissertation, Harvard University, 2000.

Fuertes Herreros, José Luis. "Como la vihuela templada, que hace dulce armonía:" Imagen del hombre y de la ciencia en el Renacimiento desde un relato de Pérez de Oliva (1494-1531)." *Revista Española de Filosofía Medieval* 9 (2002): 327-337.

_____. "Pérez de Oliva: reconstrucción biográfica." Fernán Pérez de Oliva, *Cosmografía Nueva.* Eds. C. Flores, P. García, J. Fuertes and Sandoval. Salamanca: Universidad de Salamanca, 1985. 27-68.

García Gallo, Alfonso. *Los orígenes españoles de las instituciones americanas.* Madrid: Real Academia de Jurisprudencia y Legislación, 1987.

García Icazbalceta, Joaquín. *Francisco Terrazas y otros poetas del siglo XVI.* Madrid: Ediciones José Porrúa Turanzas, 1962.

García Jiménez, María E. *La poesía elegíaca medieval en lengua castellana.* Logroño: Instituto de Estudios Riojanos, 1994.

García Soto, Claudio. "Valor, honor y fama en la literatura colonial." *Nación y literatura. Itinerarios de la palabra escrita en la cultura venezolana.* Coord. Carlos Pacheco, Luis Barrera Linares y Beatriz González Stephan. Caracas: Fundación Bigott, 2006. 51-62.

Gargano, Antonio. "Imago mentis': fantasma e creatura reale nella lirica castigliana del Cinquecento". *Capitoli per una storia del cuore. Saggi sulla lirica romanza.* Ed.Francesco Bruni.Palermo: Sellerio Editore, 1988. 181-220.

Gil, Juan and Consuelo Varela, eds. *Cartas particulares a Colón y Relaciones coetáneas.* Madrid: Alianza, 1989.

Glendon, Mary Ann. "The Forgotten Crucible: The Latin American Influence on the Universal Human Rights Idea." *Harvard Human Rights Journal* 16 (2003): 27–39.

Goic, Cedomil. "La tópica de la conclusión en Ercilla." *Revista Chilena de Literatura* IV (1971): 17-34.

Greenblatt, Stephen. *Hamlet in Purgatory.* Princeton, NJ: Princeton University Press, 2001.

Greene, Thomas M. "The Natural Tears of Epic." In Beissinger, Tylus, and Wofford. 189-202.

_____. *The Light in Troy. Imitation and Discovery in Renaissance Poetry.* New Haven: Yale University Press, 1982.

Hanke, Lewis. *All Mankind is One. A Study of the Disputation Between Bartolomé de Las Casas and Juan Ginés de Sepúlveda in 1550 on the Intellectual and Religious Capacity of the American Indians.* De Kalb: Northern Illinois University Press, 1974.

Harrison, Robert Pogue. *The Dominion of the Dead.* Chicago: The University of Chicago Press, 2003.

Hartog, François. *Memories of Odysseus.* Chicago: University of Chicago Press, 2001.Holst-Warhaft, Gail. *Dangerous Voices: Women's Laments and Greek Literature.* New York: Routledge, 1992.

Hudson, Charles. *Knights of Spain, Warriors of the Sun. Hernando de Soto and the South's Ancient Chiefdoms.* Athens & London: The University of Georgia Press, 1997.

Kadir, Djelal. *Columbus and the Ends of the Earth: Europe's Prophetic Rhetoric As Conquering Ideology.* Berkeley: University of California Press, 1992.

Kumar, Vidya. "A Proleptic Approach to Postcolonial Legal Studies? A Brief Look at the Relationship Between Legal Theory and Intellectual History." *Law, Social Justice & Global Development Journal* 2 (2003): 1-21.

Laplanche, Jean. *Essays on Otherness.* Trans. John Fletcher. London: Routledge, 1999.

Lara Garrido, José. *Los mejores plectros. Teoría y práctica de la épica culta en el Siglo de Oro.* Málaga: Universidad de Málaga, 1999.

Lasarte, Pedro. "Francisco de Terrazas, Pedro de Ledesma y José de Arrázola: Algunos poemas novohispanos inéditos." *Nueva Revista de Filología Hispánica* 45, 1 (1997): 45-66.

Lerner, Isaías. "América y la poesía áurea: la versión de Ercilla." *Edad de Oro* X (1991): 125-40.

Lida de Malkiel, María Rosa. *Dido en la literatura española.* London: Tamesis, 1977.

Lobo Lasso de la Vega, Gabriel. *Mexicana.* Ed. José Amor y Vázquez. Madrid: Atlas, 1970.

_____. *De Cortés valeroso y Mexicana.* Ed. Nidia Pullés-Linares. Madrid: Iberoamericana, 2005.

Manero, María Pilar. *Imágenes petrarquistas en la lírica española.* Barcelona: PPU, 1990.

Manzano Manzano, Juan. *Colón y su secreto. El predescubrimiento.* Madrid: Cultura Hispánica, 1989.

Mariscal, George. "Bartolomé de las Casas on Imperial Ethics and the Use of Force." *Reason and Its Others: Italy, Spain, and the New World.* Ed. David Castillo and Massimo Lollini. Hispanic Issues 30. Nashville: Vanderbilt University Press, 2006. 259–279.

Marrero-Fente, Raúl. *La poética de la ley en Las capitulaciones de Santa Fe.* Madrid: Trotta, 2000.

_____. "Lengua, imitación y diálogo en la *Historia de la invención de las Yndias* de Fernán Pérez de Oliva." *Hispanófila* 133 (2001): 1-15.

Martínez-Valverde, Carlos. "Aspectos marítimos de la conquista del Perú." *Revista General de Marina* 223 (1992): 151-170.

Mazzotti, José A., ed. *Agencias criollas: la ambigüedad "colonial" en las letras hispanoamericanas.* Pittsburgh, PA: IIL, 2000.

_____. *Coros mestizos del Inca Garcilaso: resonancias andinas.* Lima: Fondo de Cultura Económica, 1996.

Mendieta, Eduardo. *Global Fragments: Latinamericanisms, Globalizations and Critical Theory.* Albany: State University of New York Press, 2007.

Menéndez y Pelayo, Marcelino. *Historia de la poesía hispano-americana*. Madrid: Librería General de Victoriano Sánchez, 1911.

Mignolo, Walter. *Local Histories/Global Designs: Coloniality, Subaltern Knowledge and Border Thinking*. Princeton: Princeton University Press, 2000.

Morales Padrón, Francisco. *Teoría y leyes de la conquista*. Sevilla: Universidad de Sevilla, 2008.

Morton, F. Rand, ed. *La conquista de la Nueva Castilla. Poema narrativo prerrenacentista de tema americano del siglo XVI*. Mexico: Ediciones de Andrea, 1963.

Moore, Sally. *Power and property in Inca Peru*. New York: Columbia University Press, 1958.

Muldoon, James. *Popes, Lawyers, and Infidels: The Church and the Non-Christian World, 1250-1550*. Philadelphia: University of Pennsylvania Press, 1979.

Murnaghan, Sheila. "The Poetics of Loss in Greek Epic." In Beissinger, Tylus, andWofford. 203-220.

Murrin, Michael. *History and Warfare in Renaissance Epic*. Chicago: University of Chicago Press, 1994.

Nieto Nuño, Miguel. "Descubrimiento y conquista de la nueva Castilla (Un poema heroico olvidado)." *Mosaico de varia lección literaria en homenaje a José Ma. Capote Benot*. Salamanca: Universidad de Salamanca, 1993.

____. *La conquista del Perú (Poema heroico de 1537)*. Cáceres: Institución Cultural "El Brocense" de la Excma. Diputación Provincial de Cáceres, 1992.

Núñez Rivera, J. Valentín. "Entre la epístola y la elegía. Sus confluencias genéricas en la poesía del renacimiento." *La Elegía. III Encuentro Internacional sobre Poesía del Siglo de Oro*.Ed. Begoña LópezBueno. Sevilla: Universidad de Sevilla, 1990.167-213.

Nuttal, Anthony. *Openings. Narrative Beginnings from the Epic to the Novel*. Oxford: Oxford University Press, 1992.

Ogden, Daniel. *Magic, witchcraft, and ghosts in the Greek and Roman worlds*. Oxford & New York: Oxford University Press, 2002.

Ojer, Pablo and Efraín Subero. *El primer poema de tema venezolano*. Caracas: Ministerio de Educación, 1973.

Ortega, Julio. *El discurso de la abundancia*. Caracas: Monte Avila Editores, 1990.

Pagán, Victoria. "The Mourning After: Statius Thebaid 12." *American Journal of Philology* 121 (2000): 423-452.

Pagden, Anthony. *Spanish Imperialism and the Political Imagination: Studies in European and Spanish-American Social and Political Theory, 1513-1830*. New Haven: Yale University Press, 1990.

Pennington, Kenneth J. "Bartolomé de Las Casas and the Tradition of Medieval Law." *Church History* 39.2 (1970): 149–161.

Peña, Margarita. *Literatura entre dos mundos. Interpretación crítica de textos coloniales y peninsulares*. México: Ediciones del Equilibrista, 1992.

Pereña, Luciano. *La idea de justicia en la conquista de América*. Madrid: MAPFRE, 1992.

Pérez, Joseph. "El humanismo español frente a América." *Cuadernos Hispanoamericanos* CCCLXXV (1981): 477-89.

Pérez de Oliva, Fernán. *Historia de la invención de las Yndias. Historia de la conquista de la Nueva España*. Ed. Pedro Ruiz Pérez. Córdoba: Universidad de Córdoba, 1993.

____. *Historia de la invención de las Indias*. Ed. José Juan Arrom. México: Siglo Veintiuno, 1991.

____. *Historia de la inuención de las Yndias*. Ed. José Juan Arrom. Bogotá: Instituto Caro y Cuervo, 1965.

Pierce, Frank. *La poesía épica del Siglo de Oro*. Madrid: Gredos, 1968.

_____. *Alonso de Ercilla y Zúñiga*. Amsterdam: Rodopi, 1984.

Porras Barrenechea, Raúl. Ed. *Las relaciones primitivas de la conquista del Perú*. Paris: Presses Modernes, 1937.

Prieto, Antonio. *La poesía española del siglo XVII*. Madrid: Cátedra, 1998. Vol. 2.

Pucci, Pietro. *Odysseus Polutropos. Intertextual Readings in The Odyssey and The Iliad*. Ithaca & London:Cornell University Press, 1995.

Punter, David. "Spectral Criticism." *Introducing Criticism at the 21st Century*. Ed. Julian Wolfreys.Edinburgh: Edinburgh University Press, 2002. 259-278.

Pupo-Walker, Enrique. *Historia, creación y profecía en los textos del Inca Garcilaso de la Vega*. Madrid: Ediciones José Porrúa Turanzas, 1982.

Quijano, Aníbal. "Coloniality of Power and Eurocentrism in Latin America." *International Sociology*. 15, 2 (2000): 215-32.

Quint, David. *Epic and Empire. Politics and Generic Form from Virgil to Milton*.Princeton: Princeton University Press, 1993.

Rabasa, José. *Writing Violence on the Northern Frontier. The Historiography of Sixteenth-Century New Mexico and Florida and the Legacy of Conquest*.Durham and London: Duke University Press, 2000.

Rabaté, Jean Michel. *La pénultime est morte: Spectographies de la modernité*. Paris: Editions Champ Vallon, 1993.

Race, William H. *Classical Genres and English Poetry*. London: Methuen, 1988.

Ramajo Caño, Antonio. "Huellas clásicas en la poesía funeral española (en latín y romance) en los siglos de oro." *Revista de Filología Española* LXXIII (1993): 313-328.

Ramos, Demetrio. Los contactos trasatlánticos decisivos, como precedentes del viaje de Colón. Valladolid: Seminario americanista de la Universidad de Valladolid, 1972.

Redfield, James M. *La tragedia de Héctor. Naturaleza y cultura en la Ilíada*. Barcelona: Destino, 1992.

Restall, Matthew. *Seven Myths of the Spanish Conquest*. Oxford: Oxford UniversityPress, 2004.

Restrepo, Luis Fernando. *Un Nuevo Reino Imaginado: Las Elegías de Varones Ilustres de Indias de Juan de Castellanos*.Bogota: Instituto Colombiano de Cultura Hispánica, 1999.

Ricciardi, Alessia. *The Ends of Mourning. Psychoanalysis, Literature, Film*. Stanford: Stanford University Press, 2003.

Rico, Francisco. *El pequeño mundo del hombre. Varia fortuna de una idea en la cultura española*. Barcelona: Destino, 2005.

_____. *El sueño del humanismo. De Petrarca a Erasmo*. Barcelona: Destino, 2002.

_____."Reseña a Hernán Pérez de Oliva, *Historia de la invención de las Yndias*, ed. José Juan Arrom." *MLN* 82, 5 (1967): 658-659.

Rodríguez-Vechini, Hugo. "Don Quijote y La Florida del Inca." *Revista Iberoamericana*48 120-121 (1982): 580-620.

Romero, Fernando and Emilia Romero. "Probables itinerarios de los tres primeros viajes marítimos de la conquista del Perú." *Revista de Historia de América* 16 (1943): 1-23.

Romero Galván, José Rubén. "Tlantepucylama: Una hechicera entre dos culturas." *La literatura novohispana. Revisión crítica y propuestas metodológicas*. Eds. José Pascual Buxó and Arnulfo Herrera. Mexico: Universidad Autónoma de México, 1994. 111-24.

Romm, James S.*The Edges of the Earth in Ancient Though. Geography, Exploration and Fiction*. Princeton, N.J.: Princeton University Press, 1992.

Rosen, Lawrence. *Law as Culture: An Invitation*. Princeton: Princeton University Press, 2006.

Rowe, John H. "Inca Culture at the Time of the Spanish Conquest." *Handbook of South American Indians*. Washington, D.C.: Government Printing Office, 1946. Vol. 2. 183-330.

Ruiz Pérez, Pedro. "Una versión epistolar del *Razonamiento de la Navegación del Guadalquivir* de Pérez de Oliva." *Voz y letra* XIII, 1 (2002): 45-68.

____. "La realidad americana y su conformación literaria en Fernán Pérez de Oliva." *Letras de Deusto* 24, 65 (1994): 197-214.

____. *Fernán Pérez de Oliva y la crisis del Renacimiento*. Córdoba: Universidad de Córdoba, 1987.

Saavedra y Guzmán, Antonio de. *El peregrino indiano*. Ed.José Rubén Romero Galván. México: Consejo Nacional para la Cultura y las Artes, 1989.

Said, Edward. *Culture and Imperialism*. London: Chatto, 1993.

Salas Alberto, M. Guérin and J. L. Moure, eds. *Crónicas iniciales de la conquista del Perú*. Buenos Aires: Editorial Plus Ultra, 1987.

Schmitt, Jean Claude. *Ghosts in the Middle Ages: The Living and the Dead in Medieval Society*. Chicago: University of Chicago Press, 1998.

Seed, Patricia. *Ceremonies of Possession in Europe's Conquest of the New World, 1492-1640.*Cambridge: Cambridge University Press, 2006.

Serés, Guillermo. "La ficción y la "verdad del entendimiento:" Algunas consideraciones de poética medieval." *Revista de Poética Medieval* 4 (2000): 153-86.

____. *La traducción en Italia y España durante el siglo XV. La "Ilíada en romance" y su contexto cultural.*Salamanca:Universidad de Salamanca, 1997.

Spivak, Gayatri Chakravorty. "Constitution and Culture Studies." *Legal Studies As Cultural Studies A Reader in (Post) Modern Critical Theory*. Albany: State University of New York Press, 1995.

Sprecher de Bernegg, Johan Andreass, ed. *Conquista de la Nueva Castilla-Poema Eroico*. Paris: Saint Hilaire Blanc, 1848.

Subirats, Eduardo. *El continente vacío: la conquista del Nuevo Mundo y la concienciamoderna*. Barcelona: Anaya & Mario Muchnik, 1994.

Szászdi, Adám. "Dos fuentes para la historia de la empresa de Pizarro y Almagro: La 'Crónica Rimada' y la Relación Sámano." *Historiografía y bibliografía Americanistas* 25 (1981): 89-146.

Tejedor, Basilio. *La fe por la palabra. Estudios y traducciones literarias*. Mérida: Universidad de los Andes, 2008.

Terrazas, Francisco de. *Poesías*. Ed. Antonio Castro Leal. México: Porrúa, 1941.

Thomas, Hugh. *Conquest. Montezuma, Cortés, and the Fall of Old Mexico*. New York: Simon & Schuster, 1993.

____. *El imperio español. De Colón a Magallanes*. Barcelona: Planeta, 2003.

Thomson, Leslie, ed. *Fortune: "All is but fortune."* Washington D.C.: Folger Shakespeare Library, 2000.

Tola, Eleonora. "La metáfora de la nave en *Tristia* y *Epistulae ex Ponto* o la identidad fluctuante en la escritura ovidiana del exilio." *Cuadernos de Filología Clásica. Estudios Latinos* 21 (2001): 45-55.

Trimborn, H. *El delito en las altas culturas de América*. Lima: Universidad Nacional Mayor de San Marcos, 1968.

____. "Las clases sociales en el Imperio Incaico." *Revista del Instituto Americano de Arte*. Perú. vol. 2 no. 7 (1954): 21-62.

____. "La importancia de la América precolombina para la historia comparada del Derecho." *Investigación y progreso* IX (1935): 291-294.

Triviños, Gilberto. "Revisitando la literatura chilena: "Sigue diciendo cayeron/di más: volveran mañana." *Atenea* 487 (2003): 113-134.

Ullmann, Walter. *Medieval Papalism: The Political Theories of the Medieval Canonists.* London: Methuen, 1949.

Vaquero, Mercedes. "Relación entre el Poema de Alfonso XI y el Poema da Batalha do Salado." *Actas del I Congreso de la Asociación Hispánica de Literatura Medieval.* Ed. Vicente Beltrán, Barcelona: PPU, 1988. 581-593.

_____. "Contexto literario de las crónicas rimadas medievales." *Dispositio* 27 (1985): 45-63.

Varallanos, José. *El derecho indiano a través de Nueva crónica y su influencia en la vida social peruana.* Lima: Suma, 1946.

Vargas, Javier. *Historia del derecho peruano: parte general y derecho incaico.* Lima: Universidad de Lima, 1993.

Varón Gabai, Rafael. *La ilusión del poder. Apogeo y decadencia de los Pizarros en la conquista del Perú.* Lima: Instituto Francés de Estudios Andinos, 1997.

Vega, María José, "Miseria y dignidad del hombre en el renacimiento: De Petrarca a Pérez de Oliva." *Insula* 674 (2003): 6-9.

Vega, Garcilaso de la. *Comentarios reales de los Incas.* Ed. Aurelio Miró Quesada. Caracas: Biblioteca Ayacucho, 1976. Vol.1.

_____. *La Florida del Inca.* Ed. Carmen de Mora. Madrid: Alianza, 1988.

Verdesio, Gustavo: "Mapping the Pre-Columbian Americas: Indigenous Peoples of the Americas and Western Knowledge." Ed. Sara Castro-Klarén. *A Companion to Latin American Literature and Culture.* Malden, MA: Blackwell, 2008. 35-48

Vernant, Jean-Pierre. "A 'Beautiful Death' and the Disfigured Corpse in Homeric Epic." *Oxfords Readings in Homer's Iliad.* Ed. Douglas L. Cairns. London: Oxford University Press, 2001.

Virgil. *Eneida.* Madrid: Cátedra, 1995.

Weissbrodt, David. *The Rights of Non-Citizens.* New York and Geneva: United Nations, 2006.

Williams, Robert A. *The American Indian in Western Legal Thought: The Discourses of Conquest.* New York: Oxford University Press, 1990.

Ynduráin, Domingo. "La invención de una lengua clásica (Literatura vulgar y Renacimiento en España)." *Edad de Oro* I (1982): 13-34.

Zamora, Margarita. *Language, authority, and indigenous history in the Comentarios reales de los Incas.* Cambridge: Cambridge University Press, 1998.

_____. *Reading Columbus.* Berkeley: University of California Press, 1993.

Zumthor, Paul. *La lettre et la voix: de la "littérature médiévale.* Paris: Seuil, 1987.

# INDEX

Raúl Marrero-Fente is Associate Professor of Spanish and Law at the University of Minnesota. His research focuses on Colonial Latin America, trans-Atlantic studies, and human rights. He is the author of *Epic, Empire and Community in the Atlantic World: Silvestre de Balboa's Espejo de Paciencia* (Bucknell University Press, 2008).